# THE UNITED STATES
# AND CANADA

## A POLITICAL STUDY

By
### GEORGE M. WRONG
Professor of History in the University of Toronto

### THE ABINGDON PRESS
NEW YORK    CINCINNATI

# WESLEYAN UNIVERSITY

## GEORGE SLOCUM BENNETT FOUNDATION

## LECTURES

**For the Promotion of a Better Understanding of National Problems and of a More Perfect Realization of the Responsibilities of Citizenship**

### SECOND SERIES—1919-1920

# CONTENTS

# INTRODUCTION

GEORGE SLOCUM BENNETT, a graduate of Wesleyan University in the class of 1864, showed his lifelong interest in the training of youth for the privileges and duties of citizenship by long periods of service as a member of the board of education of his home city, and as member of the boards of trustees of Wyoming Seminary and Wesleyan University.

It was fitting, therefore, that, when the gifts made by himself and family to Wesleyan University were combined to form a fund whose income should be used "in defraying the expenses of providing for visiting lecturers, preachers, and other speakers supplemental to the college faculty," it should have been decided that the primary purpose should be to provide each year a

7

course of lectures, by a distinguished speaker, "for the promotion of a better understanding of national problems and of a more perfect realization of the responsibilities of citizenship," and to provide for the publication of such lectures so that they might reach a larger public than the audience to which they should, in the first instance, be addressed.

To give the second course of lectures on this foundation, the joint committee for its administration, appointed by the board of trustees and by the faculty, selected George Mackinnon Wrong, professor of history in the University of Toronto. This choice was made in hearty recognition of the closer sympathy which had drawn the two sister nations of English speech on this continent to one another in the comradeship of arms, of ideals, and of losses in the World War. It was also made in appreciation not merely of Professor Wrong's high scholarship as an historian, but also of the fine spirit in which he has ever exemplified his conviction that the English-speaking peoples, especially on this continent, should live together in friendship and work together for the advancement in the world of liberty, self-government, and peace.

WILLIAM ARNOLD SHANKLIN,
REUBEN NELSON BENNETT,
ALBERT WHEELER JOHNSTON,
FRANK EDGAR FARLEY,
GEORGE MATTHEW DUTCHER,
Committee.

# PREFACE

Lectures to a university audience should, of course, express the detached mind of a searcher after truth, and I have tried to maintain this attitude and to refrain from either praise or blame in discussing both the present and the past. My aim has been to explain, in no recondite or learned way, some of the things in which the United States and Canada are alike and also different.

Canada reads much more about the United States than the United States reads about Canada, just as Scotland reads more about England than England reads about Scotland. This condition is inevitable when a nation with a small population lies side by side with a greater neighbor speaking the same language. To the thought of the people of the United States, numbering a hundred millions, Canada, with its eight millions, does not loom large; while the opposite condition is found in Canada. Many of the books and the newspapers which Canadians read are impregnated with American thought, while Canada exercises practically no influence upon her neighbor.

It is chiefly due to this lack of reciprocity in thought that occasionally, in quarters generally well informed, discussions arise as to whether, to cancel her debt, Great Britain might not sell Canada to the United States. Such a proposal causes a pained smile on the faces of people on both sides of the frontier who really understand. England might as well propose to sell Scotland to France or Germany. Sometimes too a desire is expressed to help to liberate Canada. The only answer to such suggestions is to try to reach a better understanding of the relations of the two peoples and it was to aid, however slightly, in effecting this that these lectures were given.

I am greatly indebted to Professor George M. Dutcher, vice-president of Wesleyan University, for many personal kindnesses and to my friend Professor W. Bennett Munro, of Harvard University, for helpful criticism.

UNIVERSITY OF TORONTO.     G. M. W.

# LECTURE I

## THE DOMINANCE OF THE ENG-
## LISH-SPEAKING PEOPLES
## IN AMERICA

ERAS of excitement and passion are invariably followed by disillusion and reaction, and the days after the Great War have seen this inevitable result. Over the beautiful portal of a churchyard in England were written the words, "This is none other than the Gate of Heaven." In a stormy season the custodian put on the gatepost the notice that "owing to the inclemency of the weather this gate is closed until further notice." This is our state of mind at the present time. During the days of peace the political weather has proved inclement and a good many people are wondering whether the sun will ever shine again. The joy of battle is exhilarating, even if the fight is exhausting. When peace with victory was still beyond reach we desired it with a great longing. Now it has come. The old stimulus is gone and not yet

13

have we been able to concentrate our thoughts upon that goal in the future which will inspire us to combined effort. Faintheart is tempted to be weary and depressed.

It is probably true that the war would not have taken place if during the last ten years the English-speaking peoples had shown that they were united. Wisdom after the event is not of a very exacting or penetrating kind, and we need not lay too much emphasis upon what might have been. Clearly, however, if the vast array of power which is represented by the United States and the British Commonwealth had been used during the last ten years to say that there should be no war, its word might well have proved effective even to restrain Germany's lust for world power. In fact, as we know, Germany did not believe that the nations within the British Commonwealth would unite to check her; and it would have required something very definite and precise to make her believe that the United States could be counted upon to act with them. It remains true, however, that voices speaking in English might have preserved the world which existed before 1914.

It may, indeed, be well that that world, sick as now we see it to have been, should go. Not always is it true that in the sunlight we see the truth most clearly. It is in the darkness of the night that the stars glow and the moon shines with a beauty which may not be seen at midday. In the darkness of sorrow and sacrifice men learn to know the mysteries of their own hearts. This appears to be an ultimate law of life, and it is vain to question the constitution of a world in which we ourselves play so feeble a part. The long darkness of more than four years of war revealed to us things which we did not see in the sunshine. Both evil and good have been made manifest—good perhaps more than evil, for the war brought out a heroism and a readiness for sacrifice in the heart of the common man which we had either never known or had forgotten.

Whatever might have been done before the war, now at least we confront a realized situation unprecedented in character. As a result of the war the strongest nations left in the western world are the English-speaking nations. Possibly more even than Ger-

many is France exhausted, with a grim strip
of ruin three hundred and fifty miles long
forming her northeastern frontier.  Desola-
tion reigns where once were fertile fields,
prosperous villages, and ancient and beautiful towns and cities.  Lille is maimed; Arras,
Cambrai, and a dozen other cities are heaps
of ruins; and hundreds of thousands of the
best manhood of France lie under the white
crosses that mark the resting places of her
multitudinous dead.  Italy is impoverished;
Austria and Hungary are prostrate; and of
all the states of continental Europe it is perhaps true that defeated Germany can look
forward to the future with the greatest as-
surance.  Were it not for the vigor and
resources of the English-speaking world, we
might see again what has happened before,
that the vanquished, in the moment of his
defeat, is the real conqueror.  Long ago the
energy of the English mastered the conquering Norman who ruled in England, just as
Rome in her defeat became the schoolmaster
of her barbarian masters and turned them
into her servants.

The United States has now one hundred

and five million people. As yet of some of the new-comers English is not the language of daily life, but it will certainly be the language of their children and of their children's children. Within the British Commonwealth there are some sixty-five million people who speak English. It is thus the tongue of one hundred and seventy million people, nearly two-thirds of them in the single contiguous area of the United States. Never before has the world seen such a condition—nearly two hundred million people who speak and write and think in English, who can exchange without misunderstanding the niceties of thought in a language simple in structure, with a great range in its vocabulary, and a literature in extent and variety surpassing any other in existence. The war has brought the unlooked-for result that two great conquering peoples with this wonderful speech are, if they choose so to be, the masters of the destinies of the world.

Goethe was wont to say that, had his native tongue been English, he would hardly have ventured to write poetry, since the long line of English poets had expressed already what would have come to his mind. A people with a noble literature at their command have a great advantage among the nations. A generation without a literature from the past and limited by its own thought is indeed poor. Society is too complex for us to estimate the effect upon the life of to-day of the background of thought from a nation's past, but it is undoubtedly very great. It is true, of course, that only a few read any books but those of the present; but it is also true that in these very books is summed up the influence on the mind of the writers of all the past. Shakespeare and Milton speak through even the mediocre author of to-day. By schoolbook and newspaper, by quotation and proverb, the minds of great writers have helped to form present-day thought. A nation is what it reads more truly, perhaps, than it is what it eats.

When two peoples speak in the same language, this common influence must tend to make them alike. What is said in New York on one day may be circulated in the same form in London on the day following, and will carry with it whatever strength its inherent truth commands. It falls upon soil already prepared by a long succession of similar happenings in the past. To every point where the English tongue is spoken the thought may be carried. Be it radical or conservative, it conveys its message, and the men who read it tend to grow together in mental outlook. Counteracting influences there are, of course; contrasts of tradition and environment which involve differing emphasis upon the same thoughts; but the common language is a mighty power for similarity of outlook. The people who read both Emerson and Mill, by so much tend to come together; and when the people are those of the far-flung states of the British Commonwealth and the American Union the influence soon becomes world-wide.

In some such way we may believe was Greek thought carried from one Greek-speaking community to another. The chief endowment which the Greeks took from the home land was that of its language and its literature. The insight and the vivacity of the Greek mind working in the scene of the coasts and islands of the eastern Mediterranean were suited to the creation of small states, with no political tie other than the Greek spirit. Greece produced Plato and Aristotle, men who pondered deeply, in an environment compact enough to be understood, the problems of human life and especially those of the organization of man in society. The *Republic* of Plato and the *Politics* of Aristotle are treatises on man living under the influence of political ties with his fellows. Expressed in the vigorous and lucid language of Greece, they were carried far. They survived the ruin of the Roman Empire, they were debated with awe and reverence by the later philosophy of the Middle Ages, and they play still their vital part in the discussions of our own day. Such was the triumph of a literature in a language fitted for the expression of rich thought.

We can hardly doubt that English is the successor of Greek as the chief tongue of political theory. The most vital thought in modern political society comes from sources in the English tongue. The eternal glory of England in the world of politics is that the island state, secure in its frontiers, was

able, first of European nations, to shake off
the sway of the despot and to secure for its
people real political power. It was England
who gave to the world representative institutions, that type of political society in which
authority is yielded to persons chosen by the
people ruled, to control and in time to administer their government. It was England's
daughter who added to this the principle
which has borne the test of experience, that
free states, while retaining their local liberties, might unite for common purposes and
carry representative institutions into a union
of states in a wider nation. Successful federalism is the achievement of America. The
principle made only dim gropings in political society until the thirteen colonies brought
it into the full light of the world.

Language is the expression of the spirit
of a people and in a subtle way carries with
it some suggestion of their outlook on national life. The phases of society which a
writer chooses to emphasize reveal some
measure of its moral tone, its intellectual outlook and its political condition. Fogazzaro's
*Saint,* haunted by the problems of asceticism,

shows us the attitude of the clerical mind of Italy with which that of England has, we see at once, very little in common. Victor Hugo reveals, half unconsciously to himself, the crude and unstable despotism of the Second Empire in France which he assailed. Dickens lays bare the mind of the bourgeoisie and the lower orders in England. It is said that translations of the works of Dickens are popular in China and the explanation is offered that it is because of a subtle affinity of English with Chinese political thought, the dislike of militarism and absolutism, and with this a certain humorous decency congenial to Chinese readers. English is at least simple and direct. One of its greatest recent triumphs is the use of the word "tank" to describe a complicated mechanism of modern war. It is impossible to imagine the English calling a great avenue the "Champs Elysées" or naming a thoroughfare the "Street of the Twentieth of September."

There is no better evidence of the virility of the English speech than its changes in America. The language was matured in the settled environment of England, and it expresses the social relations of a graded society. The owner of land let to tenants is still the landlord, though for the most part there is little left in the relation which is lordly. In Northumberland the women who work in the fields are still called bondagers, but no trace remains of such a relation in their demeanor nor in their money wage of four shillings a day. On the other hand the free, new life of western America knows nothing of lords or bondage and has no need for such terms. It matures for the use of a changed society a language which, at any rate, never lacks vigor and is English in structure if hardly so in vocabulary. The educated classes in New England cultivate a precision of speech more exacting in its standards than is the language of the same class in the mother land. In all fields alike the English tongue is the medium. The most violent assailant of England, to make himself understood with effect, must in the greater part of the world denounce her in her own language.

Perhaps the most pregnant fact in modern political life is that the English-speaking peoples have become dominant in North America. Columbus was the servant of Spain, and she was resolved to have the greater part of both North and South America for herself and to permit no neighbors. Her claim to rule alone meant that any triumph of a rival would be to her own complete exclusion. Spain asked the protection of the church for her rights, and England, when she defied the church, aimed to make herself a terror to Spain in America. England's ships haunted the Spanish Main. In 1607 she planted her foot in Virginia and there remained. She too was resolved to have no neighbor, and when Catholic France occupied the valley of the Saint Lawrence, it was the fixed resolve of English policy for a hundred and fifty years to drive her out. I have sometimes wondered what would to-day be the condition of society in New England had Spain or France, and not England, finally held its coasts. There may be some doubt as to whether man is stronger than his environment; as to whether, no matter what the race, nature would not have determined the physical type. But it is quite certain that England gave to her colonies something that has made this land to-day mentally different from what France or Spain would have made it. The language, the religion, the manners of the masses, the education of a New England town, would have been other than they are had Spain or France planted here a new society. Because the English race secured final possession the traditions which go with English rule and English speech here took root, and the very spires of the churches proclaim to the air that the English seed has grown to a great tree.

America brought her own special gifts to the civilization of the world. Old things and new America offered to Europe. There were the coveted gold and silver of her mines to increase stores in Europe which had, so far as we know, received but slight additions since the days of the Roman Empire. While this was not in reality America's most precious store of wealth, it was the most alluring; and Spain, the first discoverer, spent her energies in search for the precious metals. She had no labor to export from Spain, and so she enslaved the helpless natives to do her work, and she thought she was growing rich because her ships carried across the sea cargoes of metal which in themselves would save no starving man. England was more fortunate. Her first seamen, such as Drake and Hawkins, thought, indeed, that to rob Spain's treasure ships was to touch the main-springs of well-being. The real sources of wealth are to be found, however, in those things which feed and clothe the human body and stir to its best efforts the human mind. The English settled where there was no gold, but where nature invited to the hard toil which develops character and to the adventurous efforts of those who go down to the sea in ships. Spain found her wealth ready-made in gold. England had to produce hers, and perhaps that is why the English speech is dominant to-day in North America.

Three staples of commerce new to Europe America gave to the world—tobacco, Indian corn, and the potato. Without them our present-day civilization would indeed be poorer. Columbus found the natives of the West Indies smoking and chewing tobacco

—a habit which was quickly carried to remote parts of the earth. The effect upon society of a single natural product is sometimes far-reaching. It was upon tobacco that was founded Virginia, the first English colony in North America, and from this cultivation of tobacco and later of cotton came the enslaving by the English of the Negro, which has resulted in so appalling a racial problem of to-day. Indian corn, or maize, a native American product, is now one of the most important articles of food. It is the great crop of the warm, dry, rich soil of the Mississippi valley, and it is also the chief source of human food in great regions of South Africa and Australia. The stalk of the plant furnishes, besides, an amazingly rich food for cattle. The potato, which Sir Walter Raleigh took from America to Ireland, has played since that day its striking part in human history. It too became a staple food. The failure of the potato crop in Ireland in 1846 caused famine and rebellion and ministered to hot racial passions which still burn. It caused also the first great migration of Irish to America. Not less in her natural products than in her political institutions has America spread far-reaching influences over the world.

The real struggle for North America lay between France and England. France was happy in her first stroke, for, as early as in 1534, nearly a hundred years before the founding of Massachusetts, she was exploring in the valley of the Saint Lawrence. No doubt the climate was harsh, and by so much was France handicapped. But harsh also was the climate of New England, and it had no river like the Saint Lawrence reaching far into the interior. There are four great rivers in North America draining vast areas. The Mississippi lies now wholly within the United States and became important only when an English-speaking people held both its banks. The Mackenzie and the Saskatchewan, Canadian rivers in the far north, both flow through inhospitable regions, as yet but scantily affected by the labor of man. The fourth great river, the Saint Lawrence, is the river of North America which has played the most striking part in its history. In all the world there is no other river and lake system so fruitful in its rewards to man's effort. It is the only great river of North America flowing into the Atlantic. It drains Great Lakes which are among the wonders of the world. Populous cities have grown up on the shores of the inland seas where the volume of fresh waters gather for that turbulent journey to the ocean in which they thunder over the cataract of Niagara. Where else can be found such masses of human beings on a single river and lake system? Here are Milwaukee, Chicago, Detroit, Cleveland, Buffalo, Toronto, Montreal, Quebec, and many other centers of wealth and influence. And at the portal, from the middle of the sixteenth century, stood France on guard for the ownership of a continent. By way of the waters of the Saint Lawrence she reached the flood of the Mississippi and claimed that too as her own. In the cities lying at the mouth of both rivers, in Quebec and in New Orleans, her language is still to be heard in the streets, the influence of her culture is apparent, though her political authority is gone.

America was brought into touch with the

thought of Europe just when Europe itself was experiencing perhaps the greatest upheaval in all its history.  In 1492, when Columbus was penetrating into the unknown across the stormy Atlantic, Erasmus, a young man of twenty-six, was wrestling with grim poverty at Paris and spending the uncomfortable hours in searching another unknown, the unknown of man's past struggles to emancipate his own mind.  If Columbus discovered America, Erasmus helped to rediscover antiquity and to open its treasures to an eager world.  Two years after the first voyage of Columbus a conquering French army marched across the Alps into Italy and began that mastery by the alien conqueror which if, for the time, it ruined Italy, helped to expand the minds of the invaders.  At the same time far away in the north a peasant boy with a quick mind and an inquiring faith was growing into the maturity which made Martin Luther a disturbing but vital force in the life of the age.  Germany and France and England were shaken by the explosion of new forces, and just when the fight was keenest in Europe Jacques Cartier was raising on the Saint Lawrence the fleurs-de-lis of France.

It was a great era. Its controversies haunt still our society and have played their part in the hardening processes which have formed our modern national and racial types. There were those who believed that its revived interest in art and learning and religion meant the dawn of a golden age. Thus it is that in all periods of high emotion men have consoled themselves for the imperfections of the present by the promise of the future. The day of disillusion came quickly. Before the end of the century Montaigne had described human life in its true tints of gray and brown, with high lights of radiant sunshine and also deep shadows of suffering and sorrow. By the beginning of the seventeenth century America was to Europe a solid reality, only half known, it is true, but already the scene in which national and religious passions had aroused the fiercest activities of war. Europe was torn by the bitter antagonisms of Catholic and Protestant. Spain and Portugal had succeeded in holding all of South America and some of North

America for the Catholic faith alone. English Protestants who founded Virginia in 1607 were in a sense between the two jaws of the Catholic nut-cracker with France in the Saint Lawrence valley and Spain in Mexico. By this time, however, Spain was weak for aggressive purposes and the struggle for North America lay between Catholic France and Protestant England.

As a colonizing power in America France showed what marks some of her best minds to this day, her passionate belief in a religious system based upon authority and her love of romantic adventure. In genius for trade France has never greatly excelled. The English, seeking overseas new means of living or new foundations of society which should not involve acceptance of the dogmas of the Church of England, were severely practical as colonizers. They tilled the soil, they built ships and sailed away to trade in other lands, they trafficked with the natives for furs; and wherever they settled they made themselves masters. There was little of the glow of romance in their prosaic doings. This, on the other hand, stirred many of the French,

men in some cases scions of noble houses, who
chafed at the slow activities of the farm or
the shop. The life of the forest fascinated
them. They became *coureurs de bois,* run-
ners of the woods. Past their doors at Quebec and Montreal flowed the great tide of the
Saint Lawrence coming from out the far
interior. Little wonder that the mystery of
its sources haunted them. Step by step they
explored the interior. They discovered one
by one the Great Lakes; they reached the
Mississippi and followed it to its outlet. On
into the farther west they pushed. They
reached the prairies, they saw the Rocky
Mountains.

The French are a virile race. No other
breed, except perhaps the Jew, clings to its
own ideals and mode of life with such un-
conquerable tenacity. To the French, pride
in the civilization of France and love for the
land of France are mastering passions. In
Europe through long ages they had fought
the English and in America they had no
other thought than to fight them until one
should master the other. The English were
of like mind. Hardly had they found them-

selves in Virginia when they learned that the French, long known to be on the Saint Lawrence, had actually dared in 1605 to found farther south a struggling colony, Port Royal, on the Bay of Fundy, where now stands the little town of Annapolis, in Nova Scotia. Such audacity was too much, and in 1613, though France and England were not openly at war, an expedition from Virginia destroyed this budding settlement. The Saint Lawrence was not to be secure for the French. In 1629 the English appeared at Quebec and captured this infant capital of New France. For a century and a half the struggle of one power to drive out the other hardly ceased. The English fitted out expedition after expedition against Quebec, and at Quebec Frontenac, the governor, planned serious efforts to root out the English from both the banks of the Hudson and from New England and to make Louis XIV master of New York and Boston. Of living peacefully side by side as good neighbors neither nation had any serious thought. One race, one language, one flag must be supreme everywhere in North America. On this both sides were determined. War followed war. Peace was only a truce. And at last, in 1760, the British triumphed. To them France surrendered Canada and abandoned her long struggle for empire in America.

Thus it was that the British acquired all of America north of the Gulf of Mexico which at that time was known to the world. Three types of possession had come together under one sovereignty. In the far north was the territory of the Hudson's Bay Company. It had acquired a generous inheritance, for King Charles II, by what right we shall not too curiously question, had given it all the lands bordering on the waters flowing into Hudson Bay, which meant the whole vast prairie land of the present Canadian West stretching away almost illimitably to the foothills of the Rocky Mountains. That was an empire in itself; yet was it little accounted of in the day of final conquest. Britain had always claimed it, and since 1713 France had yielded the claim. Next to this were the former possessions of the French, that vast New France in which the Bishop of Quebec had at one time been spiritual lord both at the mouth of the Saint Lawrence and at the mouth of the Mississippi. To these two territories must be added as still under British rule those fine, strong colonies which were so soon to form the United States. Never before had nation such a heritage. In all the world elsewhere there are no such areas of rich land as this realm included. It had possibilities in agriculture, beyond the vision of the most sanguine dreamer. It had wealth in iron and coal, the two great staples of industrial life. It had stores of gold and silver barely equaled in any other part of the world. In its wild life it had the richest supply of furs in the world and in its chill waters the finest quality of fish. In securing North America Britain had won indeed a triumph and to her sons and daughters that great land remains still in possession.

The Seven Years' War placed England on a pinnacle of glory. Pitt declared that when peace was made France should be so humbled and crushed that never again should she be able to raise a hand against her ancient enemy. The English type had prevailed, and there were few voices to whisper

that in human affairs overwhelming victory
has itself sometimes been the presage of coming defeat. Macedon and Rome and Spain
might all have taught the lesson. England
then had what has been called the most envi-
able of the aristocracies in history. Her
great nobles had vast landed estates. They
lived in regal palaces, waited upon by count-
less servants. Even half a century later
Horne Tooke, dining alone with the Marquis
of Lansdowne, counted thirty attendants in
the room. The great man traveled on the
highways with a pomp that to-day would
seem extravagant for a monarch. If, as
Emerson said, twenty thousand Norman
thieves landed in England in 1066 to conquer the country, their descendants had become a stately nobility, with courtly manners and the regard for nice decorum which
we find expressed in the pages of Lord
Chesterfield. Boswell, with the provincial
accent of the Scot, was assured by the patronizing Dr. Johnson that with care he
might almost be taken for an Englishman.
No trader entered the charmed circle of high
society. This was not lacking in virility, for

the names of many of the officers who fought and died on the battle field in Europe, in America, and in India are drawn from this high circle.  It was in truth for the most part men of this class who had led in the long fight which had made the greater part of North America British and forever English-speaking.

## LECTURE II

# THE CREATION OF TWO ENG-LISH-SPEAKING STATES IN AMERICA

Victory brings to nations pride and often a touch of arrogance, and this effect the complete victory of the Seven Years' War, crowned in 1763 by a triumphant peace, brought to Britain. New sources of wealth had been tapped in India, and London became more than ever a cosmopolitan center. England rewarded the men who had brought her success. Pitt soon became Earl of Chatham; Amherst, the commander-in-chief in America, was made a peer: the name, Montreal, of his seat in the country is a reminder to this day of his American campaigns. France, on the other hand, punished her failures. Lally, who had finally lost India, was done to death on the scaffold by judicial murder for no other reason than that he had failed. The civilian leaders in Canada were sent to the Bastille, and some of them were punished by heavy fines. There was bitterness in the soul of the French and exultation in that of the British. They had fought France ever since the brave days of the Black Prince, four hundred years earlier, and, at last, seemed to have her under their feet. Britain was still in thought an island with a self-complacency which tended to make her impervious to the spiritual realities of the outside world. In this hour of victory she ate, she drank, and she was merry. No other age in England had seen equal ostentation of wealth and building, such costly terraces and gardens, such outlay in collecting treasures of art. Why not? Were there not continents tributary to Britain?

The pomp and luxury of English life are, however, only half the story. We do not think wisely when we underestimate the eighteenth century in England. In that age is to be found the fruitful seed of most of the great movements of our own time. Even democracy, which has brought to us such complex problems, found its champions when London shouted for "Wilkes and Liberty." Toward the colonies overseas there was the most benevolent spirit. Both Wesley and

Whitefield carried to America their spiritual message. The people of America were, it seemed to the English, under the guardianship of the motherland which, for her part, felt for them as a parent feels for a child. The attitude of London to Boston or Philadelphia was that of financial New York at the present time to a growing town in Dakota or Montana. London should give the note. If the colonies held to it, they were right; if they failed to do so, by so much were they wrong. The colonies might not even have a bishop. That would be to confer upon them a spiritual independence for which as yet they were thought hardly fit. When they were grown up, if they desired it—and many of them feared the influence of a masterful prelate—they should no longer be under the necessity of sending across the sea for ordination the young men who entered the ministry of the Church of England. Virginia was the oldest of the colonies, and not yet in Virginia was George Washington able to secure the quality of clothes which he needed, and his supply came regularly from England. The manufactures of America were of no great moment. England was the home of manufacture. Of course the trading classes in England played no serious part in politics. That was hardly their affair. Let them look after their factories and shops, said the political leaders. The landed classes had always governed and had they not made England great? *Si quaeris monumentum, circumspice.*

War, as so well we know in our own age, produces upon political thought an effect profoundly disturbing. The man who goes into battle has faced ultimate realities and tested values. He is offering his life, and no man can do more. In this respect the private is the equal of the field marshal. War involves a close partnership and an ultimate equality of those who fight together. In the nineteenth century little Piedmont with its tiny army joined Britain and France in the Crimean War, and Piedmont's prime minister, Cavour, sat with the envoys of the great powers when the time came to discuss peace. In the Seven Years' War the American colonies had put their own fighting men into the field on a scale unequaled during any previous war in America. The officers of the regular British army considered these colonial forces as auxiliaries, in much the same way as now they regard Indian regiments, useful if controlled and directed by regular officers, but without the traditions and the training to give them any value if fighting on their own account. This attitude is always irritating to those who find themselves either despised or patronized, and it was especially irritating after the colonial forces had given manly cooperation in a great war. This irritation was one of the causes of the American Revolution.

The British tended to look upon the colonies as their property. A continent had come under British control. The people whose ancestors had long dwelt in America thought the continent was theirs and had among themselves jealous rivalries as to its ownership. Virginia and Massachusetts wished to reach out westward as far as the Mississippi; New York and New Hampshire were quarreling about boundaries. Life in America was vivid in its vigorous hopes and its alluring possibilities. The motherland had always been far away and across the sea came from her only faint echoes of the word of authority. She was inferior in that her masses had little political power beyond the indirect one of public opinion unsupported by votes and expressed often in riotous passion rather than in reason, as witness the clamor in London for Wilkes and Lord George Gordon. Boston too had its mobs, but they read newspapers and had been trained in politics by their right to vote. England was superior in that she had a class of statesmen versed in the larger problems of national policy and learned in the long traditions of political thought from Plato to Burke. In a real sense Chatham and Burke and Fox saw the world and saw it whole. There was cosmopolitan thinking in England on political questions in a sense that makes Samuel Adams and Patrick Henry appear provincial. The history of all mankind was open to Burke when he pondered a problem of state. The tragedy was that the people who, as he said, usually come to think right on public questions had no power which could respond to his appeals.

We need not wonder that, facing new responsibilities, the outcome of victory, and bearing new burdens, the debts of war, the British leaders wished, above all, security for the future. It was a part of their world outlook that they felt themselves as fully responsible for the men of their own race in America as they did for the dependent people in India. To this day Britain admits the principle that she guards the safety of every foot of British territory in no matter what part of the world. The American colonies were her charge, as in time of danger they were ready enough to claim. It was certain that defeated France would try to recover her lost territories in America. She had influence among the natives, and her agents were assuring them that the king of France was still their father and leader. The war had scarcely ended when, in 1764, there were plots, risings, hideous massacres on the western frontiers of the English colonies. Britain asked them to help with their own defense. They were disunited, heated by their own rivalries, and suspicious with their own jealousies. They hesitated, delayed, and did nothing. Then Britain, regarding the men of Massachusetts and Virginia as her own sons, in the same sense as she regarded the men of Devon and Cornwall, told them their duty, and, since they had not themselves met her appeal, she undertook to tax them. At once was it seen that they were Englishmen with a difference. They were English as Hampden was English in refusing to pay taxes imposed without their consent. But in a real sense they were not English, for they sent no members to the Parliament in London and considered the little legislature of each colony as the seat of final authority.

In the struggle which followed each side fell back upon abstract right and each had for its support some real measure of reason. It was right that the colonists, with a continent just won for their own secure future, should pay; it was also right that they should not pay except by their own free action. They were not children to be coerced by a parent. English Tory opinion considered the colonists ingrates; while colonial opinion regarded George III as a would-be tyrant and his ministers as craven tools of their master. It is not easy to understand the English political system. To our time, indeed, no one can read it correctly who does not feel the silent, secret pressure of the forces under a constitutional monarchy by which is adjusted from day to day the balance between ancient forms and traditions and the reality of power exercised by the representatives of the people. George III made his ministers his tools, and for a time, brief enough but by so much too long, was master of the government of England.

No passions are more extreme than those of a class which has built up rights on privilege and then finds its claim to power denied. Dr. Samuel Johnson was in his heart a good, just, and reasonable man, who did not know that when he spoke of the colonies in terms of extravagant contempt he was merely echoing the tone of wealth and arbitrary power in which he himself had no share. These people in America had dared to say that they could think and fight for themselves, and this seemed as ridiculous as if Hampshire should defy England. Only the pressure of American resistance and success made the great landowners who really governed England even think of what was happening in America. Never in domestic affairs had party feeling been more bitter or political intrigue more active. In such things America was an unwelcome intruder. England, after all, was in Europe, and it was issues nearer home which interested English statesmen when they gave their minds to politics. They had, however, many other things to occupy them; building and ornamentation, sports and farming. Even the Whigs did not see at first what the quarrel in America meant. And in the background was an ignorant and intriguing young ruler with a worn-out theory of kingship in his mind and a perverse and restless activity of thought which made it literally necessary to get up very early in the morning to be ahead of him. He was in reality *Carolus Primus Redivivus* in a world which had outgrown the Stuart conception of monarchy.

When a claim to authority which has long seemed, if not dead, at least harmless, once again becomes menacing, it is likely to arouse both alarm and anger. The colonies had thought that what is sometimes called the omnipotence of Parliament was only a theory, inoperative as far as they were concerned; but now Parliament claimed the right to tax them independently of their own legislatures. This stirred alarm to such a point that the colonies saw in every action of Britain affecting them some sinister design against their liberties. The Quebec Act, passed in 1774, was in reality a quite harmless measure intended to provide for good government and content in the regions lately taken from France. It granted the conquered people the right to retain the French civil law and the full liberties of their religious system. This liberality to a helpless people is, however, denounced in the Declaration of Independence as only a beginning of an effort to impose French despotism on all the colonies and to revive the horrors of the Inquisition against the Protestants of the New World. No colonial leader pointed out the humor of such designs imputed to the bigoted Protestant George III. Alarms so fantastic were fortified by the anger of wounded pride. The Virginian, Washington, regarded himself as the political equal of any man living, and was filled with contemptuous rage at any limitation of his dignity as a free man. The cosmopolitan Franklin was as bitter as Washington, and both showed a stern hatred of those among their countrymen who seemed willing to admit the claims made on behalf of the king. To the outraged American sense of political dignity the Tory Loyalists were the scum of the earth, unfit to live. Neither side in the struggle was wholly united. The English Whig praised the rebellious colonists as the truest patriots; the Tory in America was always a factor checking those in arms against the king.

Each side had one dominant thought— that of preserving a far-spreading political union. The continued unity of the British Empire is a political ideal for which many thousands of brave men would to-day be willing to die. At the present moment of victory after a long war it would prove a terrible blow to Britain's position if the British nations which have united against a common enemy should themselves fall apart. As intense was the desire after the victory crowned by peace in 1763 to hold together all the lands which were British. In America there was another ideal of unity, at first not irreconcilable with the desire to remain British. This ideal was that America should be united, that protests against the policy of the motherland should include all that was British in America and be continental in character. The Congress was from the first called Continental. Washington had a desire almost passionate to include Canada and Nova Scotia with the thirteen other colonies. One of his first problems after taking up the command in July, 1775, concerned the steps to be taken to effect this end and the twofold invasion of Canada followed. Both the British and the American ideal failed of realization. The British union was broken up. The American continental union was never created. Of the first the great republic of the United States stretching from ocean to ocean is the result; of the second monarchical Canada, stretching, too, from Atlantic to Pacific, is to-day the impressive outcome.

The continent was to be English-speaking, but it was not to be one politically.

Small seeds produce great fruits, and it was seemingly but a small thing which kept Canada out of the American Union. The American invaders in 1775 were in possession of all of settled Canada on the Saint Lawrence which lay west of Quebec. In the whole of Canada (including civilians and soldiers alike) dwelt less than two thousand British. There were, perhaps, eighty thousand French. But they felt no deep devotion to the British crown. Two things held Canada to its British allegiance: one was a few British soldiers in the fortress of Quebec under a leader, General Carleton, who hurled a contemptuous defiance at his "rebel" assailants; the other was the suspicion of the Roman Catholic leaders of the Protestant and Puritan English, who even in Congress had denounced their church as a bloody tyranny. If the masses in Canada were not alert on this point, the church itself watched and proved impervious even to the seductions of a master of diplomacy like Franklin when he went on a mission to Montreal. The

British fleet gave the final decision by timely arrival at Quebec in the spring of 1776, and then Britain remained firmly entrenched in North America. It is one of the amusing paradoxes of history that because Canada had been French it was destined in the hour of danger to remain British when nearly all that was of British creation in America broke from the old allegiance.

A new type of citizen now appeared in Canada. Ever since the blustering days in March, 1776, when many hundreds of weeping exiles had crowded on ships in Boston harbor in flight before the impending surrender of the city to Washington, there had been a stream of exiles into the lands which now form Canada. They were sad at leaving homes which they or their ancestors had created in the English colonies, and they were angry on account of the causes of their exile. Some of them were educated; the best blood of Massachusetts and New York—and it was in many cases the best blood of England too—flowed in their veins. Some of them were rough and ignorant. Because they had held to their British allegiance they had lost their property; they themselves had been social outcasts, the victims of outrage by clamorous mobs; they had been obliged to take the long and weary path to exile; and now they were forced to hew out new homes for themselves in a land of stiff forests and wintry snows. Some of them would have been glad if each stroke of the axe to make their clearings might have been a stroke at the neck of a hated "rebel" who had profited by driving out his loyalist neighbor. It was in this spirit that English-speaking Canada was begun. If the colonies were bitter against England, Canada was bitter against the colonies. In the heat of these emotions were founded the two English-speaking states of to-day.

At the heart of each of them was an idea which seemed irreconcilably opposed to the thought of the other. In the minds of the founders of the American republic was deeply rooted the conception that they were bringing forth a political creation, "conceived," as Abraham Lincoln said, "in liberty," of import for all mankind, and marking the dawn of a new day. They were proud that this system was not a survival from the past, but a new thing. Some of them felt like doing what the revolutionists in France did a few years later, marking the era by making the date of its beginning day one of year one of an epoch of new hopes and new achievements for human life. It was because this thing was so fresh and so sacred that the fathers of the American Constitution debated earnestly about safeguards and checks and balances. They feared lest designing selfishness might mar the sacred edifice which they reared. They desired that to the oppressed of all mankind a new door of hope should remain open for the pursuit of liberty and happiness. America was itself new, a continent almost untouched. Providence seemed to have reserved it for this last and greatest achievement.

The traveler of to-day who visits the great cataract of Niagara and follows the majestic river to its discharge in Lake Ontario will see at its mouth the symbols of two great historical movements. The river is the frontier between the United States and Canada and on the right bank is a fort over the white walls of which, in a pleasant setting of green trees, floats the Stars and Stripes; while across the river on the left bank is a military camp where floats the Union Jack. Here on the Canadian side in 1792, five years after the Constitution of the United States had been drawn up, was brought into being a new state based on unbroken British tradition. The creation of the new Canada had been much debated across the sea in Great Britain. Pitt and Burke and Fox had taken part in the discussion. No longer was Canada only French and Catholic. No longer could it be ruled under the despotic principles of military conquest. Fifty or sixty thousand Loyalists had taken refuge in British North America and must be given the political liberties of Englishmen. Nor could these be denied to their French fellow-citizens in Canada. Accordingly, we now have what had been New France divided into two colonies. One was to have a legislature to sit at Quebec, the other was also to have a legislature with Niagara, and later Toronto, as its capital. To Niagara in 1792 came the first governor to set up the new government. He was Colonel Simcoe, a member of the British Parliament, a Devonshire squire, but above all a soldier. He had served in America during the American Revolution and was one of the gallant band of officers with Cornwallis when in 1781 he surrendered at Yorktown. To Simcoe the American republican system was anathema. He clung passionately to the old loyalties and here he was in 1792 the leader in an effort to reconsecrate and continue them in North America. Far away in that other Canadian capital, Quebec, Sir Guy Carleton, now Lord Dorchester, who had commanded at New York until the last Loyalist had been secure in his protection, was directing another government for the French province. It is typical of the attitude of Canada toward the new republic that two prominent soldiers who had fought against the American Revolution should have presided over the political creation of the new Canada. One capital was soon shifted from Niagara to Toronto, and to this day there and at Quebec laws are made and justice is administered in the name of King George.

The eighteenth century had little experience of republics and no great love for them. Switzerland was the only stable republic in Europe, and it was a loose federation of small states, safe in their obscurity, until, a little later, they should happen to stand across the path of a soldier like Napoleon, who would then use them as he pleased. The Venetian republic had a long and notable history, but it was in the control of a privileged oligarchy and its days were numbered. That a republic could not endure was a staple of Europe's political thinking. Thus, to many, the United States by becoming a republic was taking an easy path to destruction. It was monarchy which could hold and save Canada in a system intended, as Simcoe said, to be the very image and transcript of that of Great Britain. Those were days of Tory rule in England, and, in spite of Whig protests, Canada was to be modeled on the Tory ideal. Religion, if only it were Protestant, should be endowed by the state. There was to be a landed aristocracy, and the squire was to be the leader in rural communities as he was in England. There was to be a second chamber in the legislature, where in due course the members of a Canadian peerage should sit by right of birth and rank. Stubborn conditions will not, however, lend themselves to making one political society the exact copy of another. They forbade that Canada should have squires and peers. Neither are to be found in the Legislature which still sits at Toronto, and there is not even a second chamber. A House of Lords was in truth no necessary accompaniment of the British ideal. What was vital, the continuance of unbroken tradition, linked with the institution of monarchy, remains, and one may hazard the opinion that to this day it is as strong among the legislators who sit in Toronto as it is among those who sit in London.

If the traveler to Niagara had happened to drop in upon Simcoe on the morning of September 17, 1792, he would have found a stirring scene. There were clearings along the river and already a goodly number of settlers; but, for the most part, the eye would fall upon dark masses of forest, already beginning to show the tints of autumn. Sim-

coe had issued a proclamation inviting settlers to come into his province—but on one
condition: they must take oath to support to
the utmost of their power the authority of
King and Parliament. There were already
more than ten thousand people in the province, an election had taken place for members of the legislature, and now on this day
Simcoe, as representing the king, was about
to open the first session with pomp as nearly
regal as he could make it. He could, in truth,
as far as military parade went, make a brave
show. He had soldiers enough; there was
abundance of red coats and pipe clay; and
Simcoe could array himself and his men in
uniforms as fitting as those at Westminster
for the opening of Parliament. On the banks
of the wonderful river stood the rude Free-
masons' hall where met for the time the
Houses of Parliament. Cannon boomed out
the royal salute. The two Houses gathered
in the Upper Chamber, and Simcoe read the
Speech from the Throne to the assembled
legislators. There were, it is true, only nine
members of the Upper House, which he
hoped some day might be a House of Lords,

and sixteen of the Lower House. They were plain farmers and storekeepers from homes rough enough, but they knew what they were about. One of the first things they did was to enact that English law should run in the province, and then they proceeded to provide a courthouse for each district and with it a jail for offenders. Slavery had already a footing in the country. Indians had sold captive negroes to the settlers, who found their labor valuable. But slavery was quickly ended. The old traditions of England and England's law still stood firmly intrenched in North America.

It was a far cry from Simcoe's little capital to that of his fellow soldier Washington. In this same year, 1792, Washington was elected for his second term as President of the United States. The two English-speaking countries thus started each in its new course at about the same time. Washington administered a Constitution which, as its creators fondly hoped, contained the best from every system. It has endured, and under it at the present time are governed nearly twice as many English-speaking people as are to be found in the whole British Empire. The belief of Europe that a republic could not endure has been falsified. It has borne the sternest test that a political system can endure—that of civil war. At times every constitution seems to lumber heavily and the American Constitution is no exception. Montesquieu had said that "when the legislative and executive powers are united in the same person . . . there can be no liberty," and the framers of the Constitution accepted his teaching that "power should be a check to power." The result has been that at times in the history of the United States one power has checked another to the detriment of the real interests of the nation. Congress has thwarted and defied the head of the executive government, and the head of the executive government has thwarted and defied Congress, until there has been thought of turning to that parliamentary government which in the British system makes the legislative authority supreme over the executive. In the British system, however, there has been a similar defect taking a different form. During generations the hereditary House of

Lords has thwarted the will of the elected House of Commons and paralyzed the authority of the representatives of the people. No political system can claim exemption from defects or a monopoly of advantages.

In Canada the working of the traditional British system was far from smooth. The governor sent out from Great Britain long claimed that a colony was unlike the motherland, since, in a colony, the final exercise of executive authority rested with the appointed governor, who was under no compulsion to adopt the responsible government operating in England. The issue was fought out in long and troubled controversy. In 1837 and 1838 there was armed rebellion in support of full responsible government. Not until 1849 was the principle established that the Canadian Legislature could make and unmake at its discretion the ministries carrying on the government. The prime minister then appeared in Canadian politics, as long since he had appeared in English politics, and since the middle of the nineteenth century two English-speaking peoples have lived side by side in North America, one a republic with a new type of government, the other existing under the traditions of the old British monarchy with changes, in effect, though rarely in form, which make it the expression of political forces operating in their most recent developments in a democratic society.

## LECTURE III

## THE GROWTH OF FEDERALISM IN NORTH AMERICA

In face of any new illustrations of the unity of the man of to-day with his own past some will murmur that history repeats itself and that there is nothing new under the sun. This is true of man's spirit in the same sense that it is true of external nature. All the elements are there, but they are capable of varying combinations. It is in these combinations that the unexpected is to be found. When some vision is outlined of what human society may become in the future a certain type of cynic is apt to dismiss the prospect with the remark that "human nature does not change." Indeed it does not any more than nature herself changes. In her remain always the elements found in mother earth, the sun, the wind, the rain, and the changing seasons. But, even under the control of pigmy man, these forces may be combined and re-combined, without change in their ultimate quality, until here is a desert, like that at the present moment of a strip of France, three hundred and fifty miles long, and elsewhere a smiling garden, a noble building, or a picture gallery. Human nature does not change. It, like external nature, is under the laws of its own being. But the combinations of its energies change under the control of man's own will. In his hands are the issues of justice and injustice, of war and peace, of ultimate decency or of ultimate brutality.

Pascal outlined the course of human history in his saying that "all mankind in the course of the ages is as one man who exists forever and who is eternally learning." The child is father of the man, but the man is not the child. He has passed into another phase of life, the expression of all his past. To his enduring qualities of character have been added experience, knowledge—if you like, disillusion. He looks out upon the world with a calmer deliberation, a more penetrating insight. It is a commonplace to say that it is we, and not our forefathers, who are the true ancients, for we survey the longer expanse of human action. Out of the past of man's needs and aspirations is being eternally evolved in society some new thing. In politics the English-speaking people in particular are incessantly creating fresh applications of old principles. We shall find in the *Politics* of Aristotle some of the most far-reaching principles affecting man as a political animal. The amazing insight of the Greek thinker laid bare for all time the sources in man of all the tangled web of self-interest, intrigue, idealism, and sacrifice which we call politics. He saw these operating in little states, based on the principle of slavery. He could not foresee that on the hillsides of Judæa would be preached by a sad-faced teacher a doctrine of man's brotherhood which should in time exorcise the spirit of slavery from the hearts of those who accepted his teaching. He could not foresee that when England gave the world the idea of representative government the large state would come into being composed of freemen who should choose representatives to make laws and levy taxes. He could not foresee new conditions in a New World out of which should come vast states governed under federal institutions like in some ways, and yet unlike what Greece herself had produced.

The most striking phase of modern political society is found in the wide extent of the individual state combined with government on the basis of representative institutions. It is not easy to explain why the big state has seemed to become necessary. The individual may certainly be as happy in the small state as in the large one. In the small state he counts for more and is in some respects freer, for the smaller community can give consideration to personal needs in a way impossible in the great one; it is, for instance, noticed in the United States that federal law is executed with more unvarying rigor than is state law. Perhaps we owe the large state of our time to the facility of intercourse which is possible in modern society. In earlier times in Europe (and the same is true to this day in the backward parts of the world) communities only a few miles apart had little in common and felt no need of union. Printing has brought the easy circulation of ideas, so that men who never see each other learn to agree or to differ on questions that arise. Out of such reflection comes political action on a broader scale than was possible in the days of isolation. With common ideas come movement, inquiry, and travel. The Wars of the Roses, just at the time when printing was discovered, began the shattering of the isolation of English feudalism, and out of this came the centralized Tudor monarchy, an authority unquestionably supreme over the whole land. Henry VIII boasted in his pride that no other monarch dare look him in the face. One great state made others necessary. Soon Richelieu made France a centralized monarchy, and from that age the evolution of the great state has been the most absorbing factor in politics. Representative institutions have helped to make the large state, since under them the electors need not, as in the Greek republic, come together in one place to vote, but could send from each locality men chosen to act for them.

When the thirteen colonies were changed by their political independence into thirteen sovereign states it was certain that, if they obeyed the spirit of the time, they would form some kind of political union. Among the thirteen were bitter jealousies and rivalries, but over all lesser interests was dominant the need of the big state. Complete amalgamation was neither possible nor desirable. The states were of differing types. Even in New England, Connecticut was unlike Massachusetts. When John Adams, of Massachusetts, first visited New York and Philadelphia he was as alert to note differences as is a Parisian in London. Georgia, lying hundreds of miles away, in days, too, when roads and bridges were either bad or lacking, and travel was slow, had, like Virginia, a different type of society, with negro slavery at the basis of the system. Thus it was that out of differences and distance, out of war and the danger of war, out of a combined particularism and cosmopolitanism came in America the necessity of federal union, if it was to be union at all. Under such a system the big state and the little state might be only different aspects of one whole. From the new conditions of life in America was evolved a new type of political society, which was to prove of absorbing interest to all mankind and to be copied in Europe, Australia, and Africa, as well as in all parts of the two continents of America.

Federal government involves division of power between a central government and a state or provincial government. This is perhaps its most obvious feature, but it is not the whole story. If, in some aspects, the whole controls the parts in a federal system, the parts must, in their turn, control the whole. The British Commonwealth, leaving out of sight the self-governing Dominions, is made up of states, such as the great Empire of India and large colonies like Jamaica, which have their legislatures and a considerable measure of self-government, and are at the same time under a central authority, but the Commonwealth is not a federation, for these parts have no share in this central authority. In a real federation like the United States, while the government at Washington legislates for Connecticut and Idaho, these in their turn elect representatives who play their due part in carrying on the government at Washington. Under the terms of a written agreement, called a constitution, the division of power is definitely marked. A federation, it has been said, is made, not born. It is not, like the mass of law and custom composing the so-called British constitution, a growth, which can shift from day to day the incidence of authority, unbound by any implied contract. Federalism is the result of definite agreement. Each party to the agreement has allotted to it definite powers and the legal right, defensible in the law courts, to retain these powers unimpaired. A federal system is a work of art, created and completed in the consciousness of its significance.

The framers of the American federation had one happy circumstance which made their task easier. All of them had had a considerable training in self-government, all had the same British tradition in political thought, and all spoke the same language. They could readily understand each other. Institutions do not work themselves. Those which conform to the highest ideals and are in theory perfect will work only if in the hands of men with instincts and training in harmony with the purpose of the system created. Radicals of to-day are apt to complain that the American system was created by men who had an exaggerated respect for the rights of property. It may be so; but this, at least, should be remembered, that, in spite of acute and even angry differences, they set up a new system which everyone was obliged to respect and to obey. It had fierce critics, but the critics were themselves trained in political action. For three-quarters of a century it endured with no severe shock to its stability. It may be said with truth that it is the only new system imposed in an era of revolution, with no sword drawn in civil strife in protest against its creation. Later the sword was drawn, and then not because the system was inherently unfair but because a great human problem, that of slavery, had reached the point when it had to be settled forever. It was elemental injustice in an earlier age to the black man which threatened the ruin of the work done by the founders of the republic. Never did Nemesis work with more tragic effect.

The seeds of federalism, which had grown

to so stable a result by the end of the eighteenth century, were destined to scatter far. The process proved slow. Soon after the young republic was created it was put in countenance by the appearance of the sister French republic. The cry of this republic was not for federalism. France had long consisted of more than a score of provinces so little united in spirit that they even raised tariffs against each other. Now the demand was for "France one and indivisible." The Girondin party spoke vaguely of some kind of federal union, but this only served to embitter their terrible Jacobin enemies, who gloried in the supremacy of Paris over an indivisible France; and the Girondin leaders paid on the scaffold the dread penalty of their proposals for a federal system. Yet was federalism in the air. In due course Napoleon, the military despot, came to the final ruin which was really involved in his assaults on liberty, and then a new Europe was to be stabilized. It was the idea of federalism which for the time solved the age-long problem of union and coöperation of the German states, to the extent, at least, of keeping them from making war on each other. The Germanic Confederation of 1815 was loose and unreal enough and its shadowy character has excited derision among critics. But it is well to remember that it served its useful purpose of keeping the peace among the German peoples, and, for half a century, whatever their conflicts with other races, they did not draw the sword against each other. When they did, the first act of Prussia, triumphant over Austria, was to create a new and this time a real and potent federation of North Germany which a few years later became that gigantic and powerful union known to the world as the German Empire.

The federalism of Germany was unlike the federalism of the United States chiefly, perhaps, in that it consisted of a number of lesser states grouped round one great state more powerful than all the others combined. In such conditions it is not easy to provide for the equality of standing of the separate units in the great whole. This did not exist in Germany, in sharp contrast with what we find in the United States, where Nevada, with less than a hundred thousand people, is the equal in the American Senate, which has become the more powerful of the two Houses of Congress, to New York with, perhaps, ten million people. Federal institutions, which are necessarily based on written law, depend upon the will of each of the parties to accept and carry out the terms of a contract. We know to-day that while the state constitutions in the United States have in many cases undergone radical revision and far-reaching change, that of the United States has had but nineteen amendments in more than a century and a quarter. The states have been loyal to the terms of their contract. A dominant military power, however, like that of Prussia, was certain in a federal union to use the coercive influence of its own authority and thus to taint the sources of federalism. It was not in the soil of an armed Europe nor in that of the militarist South American states that the seed of federalism took the deepest root, but in the British Commonwealth. It became the pupil of the United States, and has brought forth fruit of which its teacher need not be ashamed. And the first pupil to take the lesson to heart was Canada.

During the nineteenth century had grown up on the northern borders of the United States six British colonies, each of them with its own marked characteristics. Nova Scotia was proud to have been a British land long before Canada became British. In Nova Scotia had floated the British flag ever since, in 1710, a raid from New England across the Bay of Fundy had been successful, and what had been the French fort of Port Royal had become the British fort of Annapolis, named in honor of the dull and obstinate but good queen who then reigned. At the time of the American Revolution a new colony, New Brunswick, had been carved out of Acadia, of which Nova Scotia was a part, and which had been ceded by France under the Peace of Utrecht in 1713. Hither and to Nova Scotia had come some of the best blood of New England to live under the British flag. Newfoundland and Prince Edward Island, though alike in that each lay apart from the mainland, across a strip of sea, were wholly different in type.

Newfoundland was a colony chiefly of fishermen, Prince Edward Island a colony chiefly of farmers. Their population was small, but each of the colonies had its legislature, its civic pride, and its obstinate sense of independence. Farther north and stretching along the majestic Saint Lawrence westward far beyond the boundary of the last of the Great Lakes was Canada. The two divisions created in 1791 had in 1841 been brought together into an uneasy and unhappy union. They were in type almost wholly separate. One was prevailingly French and Catholic, the other prevailingly English and Protestant, composed, indeed, largely of Loyalist elements from the United States. Here was the raw material for a new federation, material, indeed, more intractable than that of the thirteen colonies. It had happily no negro problem, but it had the difficulty which lurks in the background of all Canadian questions—the French and Catholic standing over against the English and Protestant, and each of them powerful enough at times to check and thwart the other. By a strange fortune branches of the two most civilized peoples of Europe, age-long enemies, had come to live together in the same state in North America.

Whatever their differences these people were alike in one respect: all were devoted to the traditions of monarchy. There were none who talked of setting up a republic. The monarchy of Queen Victoria was not the monarchy of George III. Even George III had been forced to obey ministers who had behind them a majority in the House of Commons. But with the obstinacy, which he called firmness, he fretted, protested, and threatened, he intrigued to keep together a body of "The King's Friends" who would obey his will; and always his private virtues and his unbalanced and, in truth, insane temper were factors to be reckoned with by his ministers. It is probably true that the sex of Victoria led to the complete abandonment by the crown of any claim to direct British policy. Man is a masterful animal and does not like direction, in public affairs at least, by the female of the species. Under a queen the British people ruled themselves through a Cabinet of their own making.  By 1850, except in respect to foreign affairs, the Canadians did the same.  There was no longer any ground of friction between the two peoples.  They were happy in common traditions.  Probably Canada was the more vigorous in its expressions of devotion to the crown.  It had, too, confidence in British statesmen.  Pitt had broken the degrading prevalence of corruption in British politics.  The buying and selling of seats in Parliament had ended.  No doubt voters were still bought, but it was by indirect and not grossly direct methods.  To the world, to Canada at least, by 1860, Britain stood as a marvel of political purity, inciting to reverence and imitation.

Thus it was that, in 1864, when the six British provinces sent delegates to Quebec to consider the problem of political union, they were proud to put in the forefront of their ideals that they desired to frame a constitution similar in principle to that of the United Kingdom.  On the face of it they were doing nothing of the kind.  They had the dominant thought of creating a federation, while the United Kingdom expressed in its name the idea of complete political union under a single legislature. The thought of any other type of union had never seriously appealed to the British mind. When in 1707 England and Scotland had been united, it is debatable whether it would not have been wise to create a federal state rather than a United Kingdom. The day was to come for another union, that with Ireland, and had Scotland preserved in 1707 a local legislature, controlling, as every American State and every Canadian province now controls, measures which touch education and religion, the precedent might have proved valuable. The Kirk of Scotland would have remained established by authority of the Parliament of Scotland; Edinburgh would have remained a real capital, a center of political power, and would not have become merely a provincial city. Above all, the example of Scotland would have been a powerful argument for leaving to Ireland authority touching education and religion, the lack of which has been a cause of her dire unrest. The British, however, were not federally minded. By 1864 the Canadians were; and yet they proclaimed their desire to create as nearly as possible a copy of the United Kingdom.

They created a federation. But in the hour of decision some of the six colonies drew back. Newfoundland preferred, and continues to prefer, her isolation. For a time Prince Edward Island adopted the same course, but after a few years found the larger wisdom. For the absence of Newfoundland there was the abounding compensation of including in the Canadian union the far-spreading empire of the prairie country west of the Great Lakes and also the mountains and valleys, the sea-coast and the islands, of British Columbia, the latter an achievement which added softness of climate to the rigor of the eastern provinces. Just as the United States secured quickly its fruitful western area beyond the Mississippi, when once stable federal government had been created, so did Canada, when real political power was intrenched at Ottawa, reach out from the Great Lakes to the Pacific.

The new Canadian federalism showed deep-seated but not wholly obvious contrasts with that of the United States. On the surface, indeed, there was striking similarity. The provinces in Canada had powers less extensive than those of the States but similar to them. The House of Commons in Canada, like the House of Representatives in the United States, expressed the principle of representation from each division in proportion to its population, while the Canadian like the American Senate embodied the idea of safeguarding the interests of smaller units by giving them representation without regard to disparity of numbers. The contrasts were, however, real. In the Canadian federal constitution there was little detail, little definition. Power was divided between federal and provincial legislatures, organs of government were created and, in large measure, that was all. There were no prohibitions in regard to confiscating property, to establishing a state church, and to the many other things forbidden in the constitution of the United States. There was no system of checks and balances. Fictions in respect to the authority of the sovereign were maintained. The queen was, in word, supposed to govern, and an untutored reader of the constitution might imagine that Canada was still subject to the direct exercise of the royal authority. There was no mention of prime minister or cabinet and yet prime minister and cabinet were the pivots of the whole system. The official head of the state was without authority; yet in the sovereign and his representative centered the pomp and circumstance of government. Little wonder that the American people, living under a constitution in which powers are strictly defined with an effort at completeness, should, to this day, find difficulty in understanding the federal system of their northern neighbors. In one system words have their due meaning; in the other it is necessary always to explain that many of them do not mean what they seem to say. It is the difference between a new creation and a system based on tradition.

## LECTURE IV

## LIKENESSES AND CONTRASTS IN THE FEDERAL SYSTEMS OF THE UNITED STATES AND CANADA

A world grown old in sage experience ought not in practical affairs to think that an issue is solved by an appeal to dogma. In theology creeds are as often explained away as accepted in their obvious meaning; and in politics, while wise men shake their heads at the outworn solution for political evils offered in the divine right of kings, they are hardly less restive at bald assertions of the divine right of democracy. For politics are not to be conducted successfully by the mere instinct of man to govern himself. Societies there are, but they are not human, which seem to arrive at an amazing degree of organized efficiency by the exercise of instinct, without the need of a laborious process of education. The bee-hive has its skillful architects who plan and build shapely houses, its provision for sanitation and ventilation, its ordered solution of labor problems, its police, its hierarchy of government officials; and yet in this compact and industrious community we can find no trace of school or university in which the young are taught how best to perform the tasks which fall to them. Man is not so happy. Without education, a process lasting through many uncertain years, he puts little beneficent restraint upon his fiercer passions and directs but ill his own energies. It may be that the bees blunder, as man blunders, and are more dependent upon experience than we often imagine, but it remains true that the instinct of the bee leads it to achieve its ends in life by an easier path than that in which man must walk. He must plan anxiously for the well-being of a complex society. It is a vast and intricate task which no one person can understand or direct. Despots have tried it and failed disastrously. A single mind could not read deeply enough or see far enough. And now the many are undertaking to solve the problems for themselves and the road to their Olympus is rough and steep.

In America democracy has its greatest opportunity; and its success or failure in the American scene is perhaps of all problems of government the most momentous for mankind. Here was a continent dowered by nature with riches widespread and abounding, hardly touched by man. Here destiny might write some new story of man's well-being. His right to "life, liberty, and the pursuit of happiness" does not perhaps cover the whole of his well-being, for it does not express what is the gravest and yet the most beautiful thing in his experience, stern and chastening discipline in a world by him only partly known and mastered. If America was itself a clean sheet of paper, ready for man's scroll, he began there to write his story with prepossessions derived from a long record in Europe. Spain governed in America with a despotic ruthlessness, the results of which we see to-day in the instability of many of the states which she founded. From the first, England, just because her migrating sons were Englishmen, was forced, whether she liked it or not, to leave them to govern themselves, and thus, by a force working with the resistlessness of nature herself, self-governing communities grew up in America. If they were to have good laws and good administration, they must secure them from whatever fountains of wisdom they had within themselves. No one of the founders was or could become so masterful as to be a despot, so that they could not prove whether, after all, in a new world, the vigorous wisdom of one endowed with power was not better than the slack wisdom of the many. They had no alternative but to create democracies.

Democracy as now we understand the term is in reality a new thing. The Greek democracy was an oligarchy of free men in a society based on slavery, with no political power or liberty for the majority, should the majority be slaves. In the democracy of to-day all are free; and power is in the hands of the many without check or limitation. Good government under a democracy means good laws and good administration achieved, if not by the wisdom, at any rate by the voluntary acquiescence, of the masses of the people. In all the tasks which man confronts there

is none more difficult than that of so training the many minds in a political community
that they will both understand the common
good and unite to achieve it. This involves
range of vision, the capacity to see the whole,
the magnanimity to forget petty differences
in which man, a quarrelsome animal, is becoming always involved, and to unite in the
altruism of securing the well-being of others.
Power to the masses must in an efficient democracy go hand in hand with knowledge of
how to use it for the best purposes. Selfishness is apt always to be clamorous and a selfish minority, intent on using the authority
of the state for personal gain, will seek to
confuse issues so that the worse may appear
the better reason. The few who know their
minds will often win at least temporary success. This tyranny of the minority is not
the less menacing because it works with the
cooperation of the wills of those who, in the
end, will be the losers. There is no path to
well-being in human affairs other than the
path along which enlightened wisdom may
direct us, and the wisdom of the many will
come only with the education of the many.

Wisdom does not dictate uniformity of method. No doubt from one point to another there is always a shortest road, the straight line. But even the planets in their courses are deflected by the attraction from a variety of bodies. Man certainly does not take the straight line to his highest good. Politics are a never-ceasing struggle, and the man in the stress of a fight is thinking not of to-morrow but of to-day. One of the most destructive heresies of political thought is the view that what proves useful in one environment will inevitably prove useful in another. There is something pathetic in the name "New England" which the Puritan colonists gave to their creation. There could never really be a New England. The real England was a land of long traditions, its life shaped by its contact with France and other neighbors, its literature and its politics the expression of complex forces. It had the outlook of a sea-faring people living on an island, with only a few miles of open sea between them and continental Europe. To be old was of the essence of this England. But if England was old, Englishmen were young, and from their loved homeland they carried in themselves the germs of a society which feared God and honored the king. None the less did they go to a New World, and when the Old World laid a repressive hand on this new society the explosion followed of which echoes vibrate to this day.

The founders of the American republic made a constitution, and because its terms are in written clauses, subject to analysis under the rules of grammar and of common sense, we consider the constitution to be stiffly starched and call it by the inappropriate term inflexible; while to the looser British system, based on both law and custom and changeable either by statute or by new practice, we give the name flexible. The written constitution is not however inflexible, for political forces cannot be fully expressed and controlled under the phrases of a document. If a fence seems to block the way to some needed action or reform, political ingenuity will make its advance by passing over, or under, or through the fence, or by removing it. The framers of the American constitution planned the election of a president by a few men, chosen for the purpose from each of the states, but the written constitution has been flexible enough to abolish this practice in all but form and to provide for the choice of the president by popular election. The written constitution intends that the Senate of the United States shall really exercise oversight in all important federal appointments. In fact, under what is called "senatorial courtesy," the dominant political forces in each state often, though not always, control federal patronage in all but the most important offices. There is no inflexibility in respect to the surging forces of democratic life.

A group of Englishmen of a literary turn were asked by one of their number what might be regarded as the most pregnant of current proverbs. After a pause one of them said: "No one knows where the shoe pinches but the wearer"; and the others agreed as to the condensed wisdom of the saying. Each person for himself and each nation for itself must find the defects which can be corrected. The history of modern Ireland illustrates with the grimness of tragedy the deep mean-

ing of the proverb. Benevolent intentions
from an authority external is no guide to the
finding of the sore spot. No one but the
wearer knows where the shoe pinches, and in
a political society, under democratic conditions, the wearer must find the remedy.
Across the Atlantic are passing exhortations
that each side should imitate something in
the other. Federal America sees congestion
in the Parliament at London. It learns
with amazement that all governmental powers, the school system of Scotland, the char-
tering of a petty railway in Ireland—all,
without exception, of the problems in all
their phases which require legislation of any
kind, are controlled for nearly fifty million
people from a single center. The federal
man is aghast and cries: "Why do not you
create a federation? Look at us!" And
across the sea come voices which suggest
that, rather, you should look at us. "If a for-
eigner is murdered in Britain and his government asks for an explanation, we do not,"
says the Englishman, "plead that we have
no authority to act. We control laws re-
specting marriage, and do not permit any

fenced off area to flout decency by making divorce absurdly easy. We turn out a head of our government when he has lost public confidence and do not keep up a fretful war between one high state authority and another. Look at us!"

These comparisons at long range are not particularly edifying, but perhaps we may find nearer home suggestive likenesses and contrasts. A monarchy and a republic are close neighbors in North America, both subtly alike and subtly different. When the federation of Canada was made, the principle of monarchy was so much in the mind of the Canadian framers of the new constitution that they called their creation "the Kingdom of Canada." All unconsciously to itself the republic of the United States blocked the realization of their plan. The time was that at the end of the civil war. There was irritation in the United States against Great Britain, and British ministers feared that to parade a new kingdom in North America before the minds of a republican people, who for nearly a hundred years had proclaimed their suspicion and dislike of monarchy, would make worse problems already difficult. Canada in consequence took the nondescript title of "Dominion." It remained true, however, that a vital difference in the two systems hinged on the traditions of monarchy.

The superficial likeness between the two federations is so striking that Professor Dicey, an eminent authority on the constitution of the British Empire, has declared that the fathers of the Canadian system who were proud to express their desire to follow closely the constitution of the "United Kingdom" would have been nearer the truth had they said the "United States." Though a considerable minority in Canada uses habitually the French tongue, English is the predominant language in both federations. With a common language the larger country has more influence on the smaller than the smaller on the larger, for the more populous state produces a greater variety of literature pervaded with its own ideas. Few Canadian newspapers circulate in the United States, but hundreds of thousands of copies of American newspapers are circulated weekly in Canada. The United States and Canada

are alike in having each a vast territory under its control—territory of boundless possibilities.   It is said of the United States
that it has the best three million square miles
in the world, and it may be that when the
resources of Canada are fully known she
can tell as good a tale.  Each federation has
both large and small political units, though
the tendency in Canada is to divisions larger
than those of the United States.  There are
but nine provinces in Canada to forty-eight
states in the American union.

Federalism has proved the protection of
the peculiarities which grow up in communities with differing conditions.  Variety of
laws tends to protect variety of human types
and to perpetuate the influence of local traditions of character and of soil.  Man in the
forests of Maine will be different from man
in the mild climate and glaring sun and on
the browned lands of California, lying between the mountains and the sea.  If Maine
and California were wholly governed from
Washington, there would be, at any rate,
identity of the laws under which society is
regulated.  But federalism permits of vari-

ety in respect to such things as education, religion, the rights of property, and the rule of municipalities, controlled under state law. There was a time when some of the states of the Union had an established church and, if they chose, this they might still have. In Canada there is an even more striking variety. France was the creator of Canada and laid deep the foundations of her own social system. The French in Canada, extremely tenacious of the culture of their parent nation, which they regard as the most advanced in the world, have succeeded in keeping the province of Quebec prevailingly French in character. In its legislature usually the French and not the English language is heard. The Roman Catholic Church retains the privileges which it had when France was still the devoted daughter of that church, and it can still collect by process of law its tithes and the levies for church buildings made on its members. In state-supported schools the tenets of the church are taught. The system of law is French in type, based on the *Code Napoléon*. Federalism thus lends itself to variety, a virtue or a defect according to the point of view of the observer.

The two federations, lying side by side, are perhaps the most completely democratic of any of the larger states in the world. Education is widespread. Newspapers are read by all classes of citizens and carry their influence on the mind, whether it is for good or evil. Conditions in these two great unions tend undoubtedly to foster the individual's sense of his own importance. John Stuart Mill, a judge of democracy not too partial, said long ago that "every American is both a patriot and a man of cultivated intelligence." If this was a correct statement in Mill's time, we must admit that no longer is it such, but any measure of truth in it applies to the sister democracy, and in days of murmuring that democracy both does too much and leaves too much undone we may find comfort in the sense of dignity which the reality of power gives to manhood. It is something for the world that two great federations are working out their destiny by the aid of the wisdom not merely of the few but of the many.

Sharp contrasts there are between these systems. Canada presents this difference from the United States, that it was not so fortunate as to include all the territory in North America which might seem naturally to belong to it. Islands are proverbially jealous of their independence and the great island of Newfoundland lying across the entrance to the Gulf and River of Saint Lawrence has never entered the Canadian federation. The United States, so happy in the entrance by consent of all the original colonies, has had its own peculiar problems in respect to union, for the time came when states which had entered the union freely claimed the right freely to withdraw. The result was civil war on a scale to stagger mankind. Canada, on the other hand, has had no serious movement for breaking up the union. Mutterings there were for a few years after federation was achieved and before its qualities were tested, but they quickly died away. Even in Quebec, which is a nation within a nation in Canada, almost no voices are ever heard in support of breaking away.

The contrasts in spirit of the United States and Canada go very deep. The American federation was created in idealism, in the hope, as we have seen, that here was inaugurated a great human movement. Its creators believed themselves called "to vindicate the honor of the human race" in a scene where their labors should be remote from "the pernicious labyrinths of European politics." Devotion to an ideal liberty became a striking characteristic of the soldier who fought against the British, and sometimes he wore on his hat or on the sleeve of his coat a band with the words, "Liberty or Death." On every recurring Fourth of July, the anniversary of the Declaration of Independence and a public holiday forever, the assertions of idealism were renewed. A great nation gave itself once a year to the contemplation of the principles for which the republic stands. The Fourth of July oration, often flamboyant in style, often colored by denunciation of the tyranny of monarchical Britain and overwrought passion for liberty or dissolution, was none the less a recall to idealism, and tended to perpetuate that desire to remain remote from entanglements in other continents which is still a potent factor in the politics of the United States. And at the same time, along thousands of miles of the northern frontier of the United States, a people was growing into full national life who smiled, possibly with a superior air, when the echoes of American idealism reached their ears. They had no Fourth of July celebration, no annual commemoration of the right to "life, liberty, and the pursuit of happiness." Their most enjoyed annual holiday came on a fresh day in May when they celebrated the birthday of their sovereign, the descendant of George III, whom the Declaration of Independence denounces in terms so virile. These people hardly ever talked of liberty, and the alternative of "liberty or death" never occurred to their imagination. The United States was created in idealism. Canada grew out of tradition. If the causes are different, the chief result is similar. Each of the two federations is free.

The two systems are, however, unlike in their mode of working. Where custom, a careful regard for practice and precedent, is the law of life, there is likely to be hesitancy in asserting general principles. In an old society the consciousness grows up that the present is only a part and, it may be, a small part, of the record. The result is a frame of mind which we call conservative, though a better term would perhaps be experimental, a chariness about dogma, about prophesying in respect to the future, about anything but the study and understanding of the things that are. Mr. Galsworthy gives an amusing illustration of this point of view. During the war an expansive American comrade-in-arms says to an Englishman: "So you and I are going to clean up brother Boche together!" And the Englishman's answer is only "Really!" He will not commit himself to any enthusiastic program setting forth what he is going to do. In his long past he knows that many a program has failed. He will stick to his job for to-day and not say much about what may happen to-morrow. This living in the present may seem to indicate that he has no power of intellectual analysis and, in truth, in this he does not excel. His merit is that he keeps his feet on the solid ground.

Let us turn now to the contrasts in actual working of the two federal systems, one based upon idealism expressed in the clauses of a written document, the other on an Act of Parliament which is a mere outline defining powers and creating organs but dependent for its working upon unwritten tradition. We all know the chief features of the federal system of the United States, one of the most important political creations which the world has ever seen. The head of the state is chosen in every fourth year and has control of the executive government. He has, however, no control over the legislative body. Congress, which makes laws and votes moneys, does not direct the administration of the law or the actual spending of money voted. Like the President, Congress is strictly limited in the exercise of power, and a great tribunal, the Supreme Court, interprets with authority the rights of both under the constitution, which is the supreme law of the land. Except for "treason, bribery, or other high crimes," the President cannot be removed from the office which he holds for four years —no President has ever resigned—and Congress cannot be dissolved except by the expiry of the period of time for which its members have been elected. The executive and the legislative power may continue for years in acute conflict, and yet one authority has to administer the laws and to spend the money voted by the other. What the Canadians call Responsible Government (a better term is Parliamentary Government) does not exist—that is to say, government in which the elected legislature controls and can change completely the personnel of the executive power. In the legislature power is divided between two chambers, each of them an elective body, but with greater authority, as time passed, in the second chamber, the Senate, since it has special powers in respect to treaties with other nations and to appointments to office. The central government has confided to it only a limited range of responsibility, since the states have charge of all matters not specifically delegated to the federal authority, and these cover the important subjects of municipal government, public order, and education, and extend to the solemn power to impose and carry out the sentence of death. Federal courts determine suits between citizens of different states, but in the main federal courts administer federal law, state courts administer state law; and the two sets of tribunals are quite distinct in functions.

Such in meager and inadequate outline are some features of the federal system of the United States. It is pervaded by provisions for checks and balances derived from two types of motive, one to safeguard the rights of the individual states which, claiming to be free and sovereign powers, agreed to a limited union and desired protection from possible encroachment by the central authority; the other to make impossible the growth in the state of tyranny on the part of a person or body intrusted with power. The contrasts, in words at least, to be found in the Canadian federation are almost ludicrous. Here, side by side with the carefully guarded system of the United States, is a political union based upon the conceptions of hereditary monarchy. In words at least the sovereign makes the laws and carries on the executive government. An American senator, whose insight would not be praised by the wiser of his countrymen, declared recently that Canadians could not be a free people, since the instrument under which they were governed was enacted not by the Canadian people but in so many words "by the Queen's most excellent majesty." He quoted further the horrifying statement, from the point of view of freedom, that "the executive government and authority of and over Canada is hereby declared to . . . be vested in the Queen." Canadians make solemn oath to "be faithful and bear true allegiance" to the sovereign, and freely admit themselves to be "subjects" of this ruler. Little wonder that when one of these clauses, indicating the slavery of a whole people, was read aloud, a senator, startled that such a thing could be, cried out in apparent dismay, "Read that again!" Clearly, there was no thought of checks and balances in an instrument expressed in such terms.

Things in Canada are not really as bad as

---

[1] Debate in the Senate of the United States, March 8, 1920.

they seem, though it must be admitted that a nation accustomed to a constitution in which words are taken in their simple and obvious meaning is to be pardoned for some misunderstanding of a constitution of parts of which the opposite is almost true—that words are not to be taken in their obvious meaning. It is a simple fact that the constitution of Canada is the creation of the Canadian people, and that in shaping it the sovereign had no voice whatever; that the executive government of Canada is in the hands of persons chosen by the people of Canada, and that neither the king nor the king's representative has in it any real share; and that a "subject" in Canada is just a citizen, subject no more and no less to the laws of the land than is a citizen of the United States. In a legal system based on tradition and itself the product of a long succession of slow changes, old forms are retained, while into them is read a new meaning. Usually there is never a decisive moment when the old phrases have wholly ceased to be valid in their obvious sense and new phrases could be employed. There is no precise time when a man becomes middle-aged or old. The young boy and the old man are still called by the same name of John Doe, though the significance of the reality behind the name changes almost from hour to hour. So is it with a constitution which once was young but now is old. The phrases remain; it is their meaning which changes.

To the uninitiated reader there are maxims in British constitutional custom which seem to involve either irreverent jesting or statements that belong to an age when the king was believed to be really half divine. There was a time, in France, at any rate, when the statement that the highest law was the will of the king (*voluntas regis, suprema lex*) had a direct application to government; what the king willed was in truth law and was carried out as such. Out of the Renaissance period, with its bitter struggles over religion, came the maxim applied in Germany, *"Cujus regio, ejus religio"*; the religious status of a country was determined by the personal faith of its ruler. These maxims represent doctrines applied to society in their literal meaning. But what are we to say of British maxims, not the survival of a long past, but themselves modern, that "The king never dies" and that "The king can do no wrong"? The first gives a fictitious immortality to the sovereign, for it only means that when one king dies his successor at that moment begins to reign, so that always there is a king. Everyone knows too that when we say, "The king can do no wrong" we do not mean what we seem to say, that all which the king does is right. The real meaning is that, if wrong is done—as often it is—not the king, but the minister who advised action, in the king's name, is to be held responsible. Thus a statement seemingly extravagant in the attribute it imputes to the king is in reality a rather extreme statement of democratic theory, asserting not only that the king can do nothing of himself, but also that whoever acts for him must not look to the king to shield him but is to be held responsible for any evil thing in his conduct.

There is another maxim of British constitutional theory which bears on its face almost the mark of blasphemy: "Parliament is omnipotent." We know that omnipotence does not belong to man, and yet this is claimed for a body of men chosen in the haphazard of a modern election. What does it all mean? Only that Parliament has the right to overrule every other authority. This is far from omnipotence, it is in reality only omni-competence, yet the maxim does call up a vivid phase of the British system. No court restrains Parliament in the exercise of plenary authority. In the United States Congress has no control of the executive power, and if it tries to encroach upon the functions of the President, there sits the Supreme Court in solemn gravity watching to protect the President in the exercise of his powers as it will protect Congress against the President in the exercise of its powers. No organ of government in the United States has power both to make laws and to name the officers to enforce them. This Parliament does, when it makes and unmakes the executive government. The king can do no wrong, but Parliament can do what it likes, right or wrong, and there is no court to stop it, and no person, not even the king, constitutionally so immaculate; for, during two hundred years, he has exercised no right of veto, and now by the authority of custom he no longer possesses the power to veto a measure enacted by Parliament.

These contrasts in form between the constitutional methods of the American and the British systems seem on the surface so striking as to be perverse. Yet is there a real likeness. If the king never dies, it may also be said with truth that the President of the United States never dies, since from the moment that one President retires his successor must be assumed to exercise authority. Thus a republic, no less than a monarchy, has a permanent official head. There is too in the American system—if the phrase may be pardoned—all the omnipotence which man can exercise. In British states full power is given to the legislators who are chosen to represent the people; in the United States it is, under the supreme law of the constitution, retained by the people themselves. They may make in the constitution any amendments which they please. They could provide that the President should have despotic power. They could give the House of Rep-

resentatives a commanding authority like
that of the House of Commons in the British system, and they could make the Senate
an hereditary body, so that sons of senators
should step by right into the seats vacated
by the death of their fathers. The people are
omnipotent in the United States as is Parliament in England; under the reign of law,
applied no less in the United States than in
the British Empire, if the state, like the
king, can do no wrong, its servants do wrong
and are held responsible before the law for
their actions.

In the two systems it is not ultimate principles but methods of working which are
different, and here again the contrasts are
vivid. I am myself convinced that the deepest and most important difference is in a
mode of political action which, found in germ
in Britain at the period of the American Revolution, has matured since then into a clearly
defined system, known as Responsible or
Parliamentary Government. It was not
effective in the time of George III. During the war with the American colonies there
came a time, in 1778, when public opinion

in England was overwhelmingly in favor of
far-reaching conciliation which would certainly give the colonies their freedom and
might at the same time preserve the unity of
the British Empire. The man whom the nation desired to take office and effect recon-
ciliation was the Earl of Chatham. At the
present time the sovereign could not resist
such a demand. But George III resisted it.
In opposition Chatham had attacked the policy which the king chose to consider not that
of his ministers but of himself. He hated
Chatham with a bitter and sullen hatred, and
now he declared that he would not have
Chatham as his chief adviser; rather than
submit to this slavery he would resign the
crown. The king was able, by his control of
a Parliament not responsive to public opinion, to keep Chatham from office, and the
result was that the American war went on
to the bitter end. Twenty-five years later
George III did the same thing and refused
the request of William Pitt, Chatham's son,
that Fox, a leader of the opposition, should
be given office. Though already Parliament
made and unmade ministers, the king could

still keep from office a man desired by the
nation. It is not so now. The king cannot
resist the demand of public opinion, and
within twenty-four hours both the governing
personnel and the policy of the state can be
wholly altered. To test public opinion a
general election may take place at any time,
and in both Great Britain and Canada two
actually have occurred within little more than
a year. No British government is safe
for an hour if it has lost the support of public opinion. It may, of course, cling to office,
but it has no security. A breath of public
opinion may at any moment blow out the
flickering light of a discredited ministry. If
public opinion is fickle, this power may involve danger. In fact, governments last in
England about as long as they do in the
United States.

This is Parliamentary Government, and
time has shown it to be the most striking
characteristic of the modern British system.
France, having tried nearly every other type
of administration, at last resorted to Parliamentary Government under the Third Republic, with the result that, while ministries

have changed with dismaying frequency, the republic itself has endured for half a century. Italy has adopted it and, in spite of difficulties almost overwhelming, maintained stability during the Great War partly by changing her ministers to meet current demands of public opinion. Results may or may not vindicate Parliamentary Government. That is not the point under discussion. The fact remains that on this method the two great branches of the English-speaking peoples are at opposite poles. Britain has adopted it, and ministries and Parliaments change from day to day. The United States has not adopted it, and the executive and the legislative authority endure for fixed periods of time and are irremovable.

The system of Parliamentary Government has had far-reaching results on British political methods. It has involved recognized permanent leaders of political parties. Here too, though, like the creation of Parliamentary Government, the system is sanctioned only by custom, and not by law, is one of the vital differences between federalism in the United States and federalism in Canada.

In the United States candidates for the presidency are chosen anew in each fourth year, and the person elected becomes the party leader for the succeeding political campaign. At short and fixed intervals the struggle for political leadership is renewed, and the program, the so-called platform, of the party is drawn up. The successful party usually, but not always, has a leader in the President during his term of office, but his authority wanes or grows strong with the prospect of his nomination for a second term. All the time the chairman of the National Committee of each party is watching and directing party policy. In a sense each of these persons leads his party, but the kind of leadership is different from that of a party leader who will himself take office and carry out his own policy. Under the British system a party always has this type of leader. He sits in Parliament, face to face with the rival leader. Isolation or seclusion is impossible. He is there to be questioned and criticised from day to day. The practice has gone so far in Canada that the leader of the opposition party in Parliament is paid a salary.

The leadership of a single man may long endure. Sir John Macdonald led the Conservative party in Canada for nearly forty years, and Sir Wilfred Laurier led the Liberal party continuously for the thirty-two years prior to his death in 1919. Each of these leaders was prime minister and the real ruler of Canada for periods longer than the as yet unreached three terms of an American President. There is no doubt that, with permanent leaders, changes in policy are made more gradually and with less friction than is found when both a leader and a policy have to be chosen at the same time. On the other hand, long tenure of a post tends to make its holder unreceptive and sometimes despotic. In England governments do not, as a rule, last longer than six or seven years at most, and the average is much shorter. In the United States their duration is strictly limited by the constitution. In Canada they tend to last too long, owing largely to the difficulty of arousing public opinion in a population scattered over a vast area.

Under the Canadian, which is the British, system, the only persons chosen by election are the members of the legislature. This principle applies in the federal system of the United States, except in respect to the office of the President. In the state governments, however, secretaries, treasurers, auditors, and even judges are, in varying degree, according to the constitution of each state, chosen by popular vote. In the British system the members of the cabinet, that is to say, the chief executive officers of the government, from the prime minister, who is really the Canadian equivalent of the President, to the least important member of his government, must have seats in the legislature, and there give an account of the administration of their offices. To take part in the work of legislation is often an irksome duty for men weighted with complex matters of administration, but it has come to be regarded as indispensable to the working of parliamentary government. In Canada no legislature is chosen for a period of less than four years, and the federal House of Commons is chosen for five years. The long term is safe enough when, in response to public opinion, an election may take place at any time, but it would not commend itself in the United States, with the member free from attack in his seat for a fixed period. In Canada, as in England, the government is dominated by a single chamber, the House of Commons, whose will the second chamber is, in the long run, impotent to resist. It would be impossible to have two chambers of equal authority and at the same time to have parliamentary government, since, in such a case, a deadlock between the two houses might prevent an appeal to the people. "You might as well attempt to stick a dog's tail on a lion's back" as to have a strong second chamber with parliamentary government, said Joseph Howe, of Nova Scotia, and Great Britain has found that she must have a weak House of Lords if the country is to be ruled under the public opinion of a democracy. The contrast with the strength of the American Senate is striking.

In the Canadian federal system there are restrictions on the authority of the provinces which stand in contrast with the rights of the states in the United States. In a certain sense the forming of the Canadian federation

involved the breaking-up of an earlier union
as much as it did the creation of a new one.
The older Canada, consisting of the two
great provinces which are now Ontario and
Quebec, had existed for a quarter of a century under a single legislature in which
French and English members were about
equal in number. There was intense racial
strife and, in the end, federation was a refuge
from an unhappy union. In such a case it
was easy for the constitution builders to
delegate to each of the new provinces only
the matters which had chiefly caused friction
—religion and education—and with these the
other affairs of a local character. Thus it
has come about that in Canada the provinces
have only the powers specifically delegated
while the central government retains all other
authority. This principle, so sharply in contrast with that applied in the United States
of giving limited and specified powers to the
federal government while the states retain
all the rest, has made it natural in Canada
to have a common criminal law for the whole
country, and a single judiciary, which admin-
isters both federal and provincial law. No

judges are either appointed by the provinces or elected in Canada. All judges are named by the federal government. Yet, except in the cases of the judges of the federal Supreme Court and the single judge of the Exchequer Court, which deals with the financial relations of the federal and the provincial governments, all the judges of Canada are paid by the provinces in which they exercise their functions. It has been the federal government which has vindicated the sanctity of the law in the more unsettled regions, and this has resulted in so strong a preservation of order that lynching is unknown. Only the federal government can exercise the prerogative of pardon. No criminal undergoes anywhere in Canada the sentence of death without the gravest consideration of his case by the central federal authority. One important contrast in the two systems depends only on practice and has no inherent necessity. Canada has copied the system of England and has the budget control in finance. Only the government of the day can propose the expenditure of public money. Each year the Minister of Finance submits an elaborate statement of expected income and expenditure, and no additions to the proposed expenditure can be made without the consent of the government. At this moment there is keen discussion as to whether the United States should adopt this budget system.

To point out contrasts in the sense of suggesting that a good practice in one country would of necessity work amid different conditions in another is to be guilty of the arch-fallacy in politics that what works anywhere will work everywhere. Would the British Cabinet system under parliamentary government work in the United States? We do not know; it is one thing to work a system in a compact and crowded island where every one, through an active press, can ponder on the same day the same political problems, and quite another to apply successfully such a system in an area thirty or forty times as great, with varying climates, a large part of the population scattered and remote, and communications often slow and difficult. In the island public opinion is alert and united because it is easy to appeal to the many at almost the same hour. But it is not so easy

to get California to ponder the problems of
Maine, or, in a different scene from that of
Maine, to understand conditions which may
be alien to the thought of its people. There
is a comforting maxim in the moral world
that each of us gets the lot which he deserves.
It may be true of nations that each matures
the system best fitted to its own conditions.
At any rate, nothing is more certain than that
it is rarely wise to transfer the system of one
country to another. Political philosophers
are fond of saying that Great Britain would
do well to adopt the federal system of the
United States. Yet it is clear that as yet all
practical steps to carry out such a plan have
seemed to fail, and that to-day Ireland, supposed to be able to find the solution of its
heart-breaking discords in a federal union
with Great Britain, is coldly critical of such
proposals.

## LECTURE V

## THE PLACE OF CANADA IN THE BRITISH COMMONWEALTH

THE United States and Canada, speaking the same language, occupy the greater part of a vast continent, and it is of some import to mankind that they should understand each other. Yet in this there are peculiar difficulties. The most vivid historical recollection of the people of the United States is that once they were colonies of England, and that after a long and cruel war they established their independence and united to form a republic. To them the relation of parent to daughter state is the relation of superior to inferior, of a patronizing and protecting society to one that is as yet immature and weak. It must be confessed that there is in history abundant justification for this interpretation of the imperial relation. If, however, it were the whole story, there would be at the present time no British Empire, except in the sense of a conquering England holding some scattered islands and naval stations and the territory which her legions had mastered. France and Holland still have great possessions overseas; but they are not states inhabited by French and Dutch who have migrated from the motherland. They are literally possessions, with alien peoples, who, no doubt for their own good, are, in the ultimate analysis, held in obedience to the master state by military power. No communities composed of the flesh and blood of the motherland will ever be satisfied with an inferior status. Spain lost her colonies because the Spaniard in America would not be subordinate to the Spaniard in Europe. The only other great colonizing power has been Great Britain. She lost her American colonies because she demanded their obedience. On the same condition she would in time also have lost Canada and Australia. There remains a great British state because of the growth of a different type of relation.

So far as the self-governing nations of the British Commonwealth are concerned, there is now really no such thing as a British Em-

pire.   An empire, one would suppose, is a
state which has a central controlling government.   But although the British Parliament is, in a strictly legal, though not constitutional, sense, supreme over all British
dominions, there is no central government
for the whole British Empire.   The Parliament of Great Britain has no constitutional
right to pass any measure affecting the government of Canada, except merely as regis-
tering Canada's own decisions.   No one body
can tax the British Empire.   Canada and
Australia and New Zealand and South
Africa are not governed from London, nor
have they any common government.   Each
of these nations governs itself.   As long ago
as in 1859, when Canada imposed a tariff on
British goods and the government at London
protested, there was no uncertain sound
about the reply of Canada.   It asserted "the
right of the Canadian Legislature to adjust
the taxation of the people in the way they
deem best, even if it should unfortunately
happen to meet the disapproval of the Imperial Ministry."   It is more fitting to describe as a "Commonwealth" than as an

"Empire" the state in which the different parts are so completely self-governing.[1]

The most interesting growth in the British Empire during the nineteenth century was in the self-government and individuality of the various British peoples. There was very little of it in the British Empire of a hundred years ago. The American Revolution removed from the Empire the only element overseas that could make any claim to self-government. After that tragic cleavage between the English-speaking peoples, almost none of British origin were left outside the homeland. In Canada, even including the Loyalist refugees from the revolted colonies, there were fewer than one hundred thousand. The same is true of the West Indies, relatively more important then than now. In India there were perhaps half this number. And this was the whole tale of British people overseas. Australia, New Zealand, South Africa, as we know them, did not then exist. There is little wonder that

[1] This and succeeding paragraphs are, with some modifications, taken from an article by the author on "The Growth of Nationalism in the British Empire" in *The American Historical Review*, October, 1916.

the successful revolutionists of the United States should feel a fine scorn of the Britons in Canada who would not join them. These seemed to be misguided supporters of a lost cause. A tyrannous motherland had forfeited all right to the allegiance of her sons overseas, and successful revolution called the Canadians craven, since they did not join in the fight for liberty.

It was, indeed, in the half-century after the Revolution that there was a real and united British Empire, for every part of it was governed from London. It is true that never after her loss in America did Britain attempt to tax her colonies. They were to her a costly burden. What we now know as the Dominion of Canada consisted of four or five detached provinces, each insignificant, each really ruled by a governor sent out from England, each backward and almost stagnant. Little thought as yet had any of the colonies that they were new nations, with the same rights of self-government which Britons at home possessed. Yet was there a something working in these communities which had promise for the future. Each of them had its own legislature; each had the storm and tumult of elections, in which there were free speech and free voting. The elected members, however, did not control the executive government; that was the affair of the governor and of the Colonial Office in London, which appointed him.

With the growth of population came changes. By 1830 there was a clamorous demand in Upper and Lower Canada for complete control by the people of their own local affairs. The controversy was violent. In 1837 and 1838 it led to armed rebellion by the radical element which asked for full political rights. Though the rebellion was put down, the cause apparently lost was really won. A dozen years later, that is by the middle of the century, every British community in North America had secured control of its own affairs. The movement spread to other continents. Australia followed quickly. Canada was the older British dominion and naturally led the way, but the British colonial system as a whole was changed, and by the mid-century its self-governing states in all parts of the world were really freer than had been the former English colonies in America.

This very change, however, brought a danger to the British system. Why should the motherland take any trouble to preserve a tie with communities which brought her little advantage? They erected hostile tariffs against her goods, they were a charge upon her revenues, they were perennially relying upon her army and fleet for defense. Canada was frquently involved in disputes with the United States. In 1837-1838 there were frontier incidents which might well have caused war. A few years later there was the question of the boundary line in Maine. Then came that of the western boundary, with the insistent demand of American pioneers in the west of "Fifty-four forty or fight," which meant that all south of this degree of latitude should go to the United States on penalty of war. There is perhaps not much wonder that British statesmen should have thought a self-governing empire overseas not worth having. Gladstone told Goldwin Smith that the cession of Canada to the United States would not be an impossible compensation to the North if the South should break away. Beaconsfield, Gladstone's great rival, hoped at one time that the troublesome colonies would become independent. When this was done Britain would be left with no European peoples overseas, but only with races of alien blood and faith whom she could really rule.

Then, just when these depressing views were current, a strange thing happened. The half-torpid colonies in North America suddenly revealed a new life and a new wisdom. They shook off their narrow isolation and formed a great federation. Fear had much to do with it. The United States, recently torn by civil war, was likely to become a great military nation, a menace to the British communities on its northern border. Because of this and of impotence and deadlock in their own political affairs, the British colonies united to form one great state. By 1872, the union of once separated colonies extended from the Atlantic to the Pacific. In this movement, if men could have read it aright, was the birth of a new conception of the British Commonwealth. But this meaning was not seen at once. For a long time the old idea of the subordination of the colonies to the motherland still survived. But the movement for separation was quickly checked. It was one thing for British statesmen to look on blandly while a few scattered colonies broke away; but quite another thing to let a country like Canada go with four million people. After all, trade tended to follow the flag, and thus, even on lower commercial grounds, it would be a bad thing to end the colonial relation. Other reasons there were, too, and one of them, most potent of all, was that, even though Great Britain might be willing to let go of Canada, Canada had no wish to let go of Britain.

Here we come upon one of the unexpected things in this strange British Empire. The old assumption was that when the new states were strong enough to stand alone they would wish to do so and would break away from the mother country. But this represented only the coldly intellectual view of politics. In fact, political loyalties have as much to do with the heart as with the head. It never occurred to the average Canadian, even when his country reached national stature, that he could not remain both a Canadian and a Briton. The British flag had always been his. Why should he change? True, he was a Canadian first, for Canada was the country he knew. Britain he had probably never seen, and he understood but little of a state of society in which there were an aristocracy, a House of Lords, and an established church. Still he saw no reason why he should break with the old home of his race and no movement for separation would come from him.

There was too a strong political drift against change. Union was in the air when the federation of Canada was created. This event followed immediately upon the reunion of the United States after the Civil War. The North-German Confederation was formed in the very year in which the British North America Act, creating the Dominion of Canada, passed the British Parliament. Three years later Italy was finally united. In the next year, 1871, came the creation of the German Empire. This was followed quickly by an eager ambition among Euro-

pean states to secure colonies.  Trade rivalries were keen, markets were needed, and
markets under the same flag seemed to be
more secure than markets under an alien flag.
It thus happened that the ungracious per-
mission offered to the colonies about 1860
that they might go when they liked, and the
sooner the better, had become by 1890, thirty
years later, the rather nervous fear that they
might take themselves off and leave Great
Britain to a lonely sovereignty over a dependent empire ten times more populous
than herself.

During all this time the movement was
growing for unions within the Empire on
the lines of the Canadian union.  In 1900
the six Australian states united to form a
great Commonwealth.  Most wonderful of
all, less than ten years later, the four colonies of war-worn South Africa formed a
strong union more centralized and consoli-
dated than any of the other unions in the
British Empire.  In no case, however, was
union effected with the view of breaking
away from the Empire.  Rather was the design to draw closer together.  Yet each union

represented a distinct type and was brought about in conformity with local conditions. Here, then, is the paradox which is characteristic of the British nations—the more they become separate in type the more they hold together.

The unity of outlook with Great Britain was tested in Canada in 1899, when the South African War broke out. The people of Canada accepted without reserve the British view of the issue and thousands of Canadians fought on the veldt. Britain, however, paid the bill. Canada was not a real partner. It was the Great War, begun in 1914, which brought to a head a long process of development. Complete self-government in respect to domestic affairs Canada had had for nearly three-quarters of a century. There remained, however, this lack of full national life, that she had no direct diplomatic relations with other states. The government of Canada had no power to deal with the government of the United States; a treaty made in reality between the United States and Canada was in name between the United States and Great Britain.

When, during the war, a Canadian War Mission was sent to Washington this difficulty was overcome by the subterfuge, humiliating in form if hardly so in fact, that the Mission might deal with the departments of the government of the United States but not with that government itself. Canada was not classed as an American nation, with the result that when a Pan-American Congress came together the American state which ranked in importance next to the United States had no place. Before the war it was uncertain what part self-governing states like Canada and Australia would take when Great Britain became involved in a struggle which should tax her full strength. The breathless days of the summer of 1914 settled this doubt. Then it became clear that on a vital issue the whole British Empire would act together. No nation was more surprised than Britain herself by the completeness of the union of hearts.

This war was Canada's first war. Never before had she recruited and paid her own armies in a great struggle. People careless of speech sometimes say that Canada went into the war to help England; but this was not really the thought of the Canadian people any more than it was that of the Scottish people. What the British peoples felt was that they were fighting together as partners. Fears there were in Canada that her civilian soldiers might not be able to bear the test of war against the greatest military power in the world. But before a year of war had passed this fear was gone. As the war lengthened world-wide organization of British effort became necessary. In March, 1917, a Conference on the War of representatives of the whole British Empire was held in London, and at the same time the direction of the war was put in the hands of a new body called the Imperial War Cabinet, in which sat the British, the Canadian, and other prime ministers. Mr. Lloyd George was careful to say in the British House of Commons that the status of the members of this Cabinet was one "of absolute equality." In the absence of the prime minister of Great Britain, the prime minister of Canada presided, since Canada ranked as second among the self-governing states

of the Empire.   Each of these states was
by official pronouncement declared to be "an
autonomous nation."   When peace was to
be negotiated it was the British Empire Del-
egation, with Canada playing an important
part, which directed British policy.   Thus
within the British Empire equality of status
between Canada and Great Britain was fully
recognized.   It remained, however, to record
international recognition of this fact.   This
was done when peace was made.   Plenipotentiaries of Canada signed the peace with
direct official authority from the king to sign
for Canada, exactly as plenipotentiaries of
Great Britain signed with official authority
from the king to sign for Great Britain.
This was the culminating official act in a
great political movement.   The British Empire had become a Commonwealth of Nations, and each of the nations was entitled to
the fullest expression of its national life.

Usually the full meaning of a great constitutional change is not immediately apparent.   Unless there is the upheaval of revolution the old machinery goes on working.
There are things which still seem to indicate

that Canada is in a state of tutelage to Great Britain, and these things will disappear only slowly as occasion arises to consider and discard them. The head of the Canadian nation, acting for the king, is called the Governor-General; he is appointed by the British government, and, in some measure, he is an official of the Colonial Office. In fact, he is not a governor but a viceroy, with only the authority in Canada which the king has in England; in fact, while he is appointed by the government in London, it is only with the approval of Canada; in fact, too, the Colonial Office has no authority in Canada, for the prime minister of Canada and the prime minister of Great Britain take counsel together and reach decisions on the important questions between the two countries. Canada has no Foreign Office, and, as yet, no ambassadors. But she has now the full constitutional right to create both when she so chooses. In the strict letter of the law Canada is at war when Great Britain is at war; but the events connected with the peace treaty made her separate consent to peace necessary and this may involve the corollary that she is not at war without her specific consent.  Far-reaching, indeed, will be seen to be the constitutional changes of the period of the Great War.

It is to be expected that when the experience of a few years has shown that Canada has her special interests in foreign affairs and is not content to be merely the pupil of Great Britain, there will be some friendly cleavage between the two countries.  Great Britain has so long controlled the foreign policy of the British Empire, with undivided responsibility, that she may well feel surprise and even resentment at Canada's assertion of variant views.  When Canada, as an American nation, takes her place in the assembly of the League of Nations she will stand more for the American than for the European view of world policy.  In respect to Japan, Canada's interests are rather those of the United States than of Great Britain.  Such differences of opinion will, however, be wholesome.  They will tend to prevent Great Britain, after all a world state with vital interests in every continent, from being too   completely   dominated   by   interests merely Asiatic or European. At the same time Canada, drawn out of obscure isolation, will learn to understand the burdens of a great Empire. The result ought to be a better understanding all round. The British nations are really closer together in 1920 than they were in 1850, chiefly because in the intervening seventy years they worked out the same ideals of political liberty. Another cycle of years may see them united in sharing the same responsibilities in a world commonwealth, and, if this result is to be reached, it will be along the path of bearing, each state for itself, the responsibilities of British nationhood.

There is no doubt that variety of environment tends to produce a variety of peoples. The Canadian is different from the Australian, and both are different from the Englishman. The differences are physical and they are also mental. The man who has seen the society about him created in his own generation will have a view of social relations different from that of a man born into a highly organized society, with ancient buildings, traditions, and gradations of rank. It is easier for an Englishman than it is for a Canadian to show deference and respect. The Canadian, in turn, is a citizen of a lesser state, and is humbled commercially by contact with a great neighbor much more highly organized than himself. The Australian, supreme in his lonely continent in the Southern Sea, has no old local traditions and no neighbors. He creates his own standards and believes in himself. When shown Westminster Abbey he may murmur, "Ah, but you ought to see the Presbyterian Church at Ballarat!" He is subtly different from the other types. The difference is not racial, for the race is the same. It is the difference caused by conditions, and it will increase with time. You will not flatter the Australian by calling him an Englishman. He wishes to be known as what he is, an Australian. In this respect his nationalism is complete.

This, however, is not the whole story. This man, so thoroughly himself in his southern home, is passionately a Briton and one in feeling with all other Britons. The thoughtful Australian or Canadian will deny that he owes any loyalty to the British Isles. He

feels this no more than the Englishman feels
loyalty to Canada.  Each of them is satisfied
to be loyal to himself and they hold together
because, on great national issues, they have
the same outlook.  I am a little puzzled when
I try to explain why this unity exists.  No
doubt it is largely the result of education, of
habitually surveying questions from a certain point of view.  Probably its deepest
cause lies in unbroken tradition.  Each of us
is set in the midst of a system in which many
forces are uniting to shape our conception
of life.  British political liberty has had a
slow growth.  The religious outlook, the
education, the social relations, the tastes and
habits of to-day come to us from a long past.
In some such way as this is the note struck
that we call British.  All the people of the
scattered British Commonwealth share it,
and, though there are different types, widely
separated, they have the unity of a family.

This unity is not racial.  Racial unity is
necessarily limited to those whom birth has
made members of the race.  Thus it cannot
become comprehensive and cosmopolitan.
It tends to run to pride and arrogance, to

thoughts like those of the Hebrew that his race is the chosen of God. When the British Empire was younger we used to hear about the triumphant destiny of the Anglo-Saxon race. At one time we seemed to seek uniformity, partly, perhaps, because we assumed unity of race. It was held that political wisdom required in Canada and in Australia an exact copy of Britain. Canada, as we have seen, was to have a House of Lords and an established church. Experience, the true teacher, dispelled this dream. In time not likeness, but diversity, of institutions was emphasized, and little thought was given to race. We know now that no one part of the British Empire can be quite like any other part. When we ask why, the answer is that this is the fruit of liberty. Nature herself is infinitely varied and, when men are free, when they adjust themselves to the varieties of nature, they evolve differences. To-day no wise statesman has any thought of trying to Anglicize the British Empire. The wonder-worker is not race but liberty. Let us dismiss forever the superstition that there is any magic in race to hold peoples together and effect political unity. In the late war the most determined and irreconcilable opponents were states of the same Teutonic race. It is partnership in common liberties which unites people.

Without including annexations due to the war, the British Commonwealth represents about one-fourth both of the population and of the area of the world. The population of the world is about 1,800,000,000; the area some 51,230,000 square miles. The British Commonwealth is nearly evenly divided between the northern and the southern hemispheres. Two-thirds of it are in the east and only one-third is in the west. The chief seat of power is in the west, but six-sevenths of the people under British sovereignty are not Europeans. The proportion of people of European origin is likely to grow, since they hold for occupation nearly two-thirds of the whole area of the British Commonwealth, with vast unoccupied spaces still to be peopled. It is a vital characteristic of the British system that, in spite of the recent war, it is becoming less and less occupied chiefly with Europe. It is of the east as well as

of the west and of the south as well as of
the north.  It is less a creation than a
growth, a growth out of conditions and ne-
cessities into a system unprecedented in the
history of the world.  It has become a micro-
cosm of the world itself.  It includes people
of every race and of every creed.  No other
state has ever held such vast areas in every
continent—almost half of North America,
much of fertile Africa, nearly the whole of
Australasia, and a great area in Asia.  In
Europe alone is the territory of the Commonwealth comparatively small in magni-
tude.  There are in it more than three times
as many Hindus and nearly twice as many
Moslems as there are Christians.

"If the Canadians loved liberty," said an
American senator recently,[1] "they would not
stay under the British flag."  Virginia and
other States desired to withdraw from the
American union and were retained within
it by force of arms.  Canada, free to go, stays
in the British union.  She is freer to go than
was Virginia, but she remains under the
British flag.  One reason is her pride in be-

[1] Debate in the Senate, March 8, 1920.

ing a member of a great Commonwealth.
Let me ask Americans a question. If the
republic, in the slow growth of years, had
founded kindred republics in every continent, had fostered and protected them, had
dreamed dreams about what this union of
free peoples would do for mankind, would
you willingly let this union end in disrup-
tion? To-day British citizenship is wonderful, for it makes the Briton at home in every
continent. Suppose that an American, sail-
ing eastward, found himself in another
United States in Europe under the Stars
and Stripes. Suppose that he went on by sea
and found himself in South Africa and still
in the United States under his own flag.
Suppose that he sailed on and found himself in India with more than three hundred
millions of people still under the Stars and
Stripes. Suppose that he went on to the
great continent of Australia and found still
his flag, on to New Zealand, on still across
the Pacific to America, where he has his
home, half a continent still under the Stars
and Stripes. In every one of these states he
has been a citizen, needing no change of alle-

giance in order to vote. And this is the British Commonwealth.

In this Commonwealth there is, as I have said, no one central government. The tie which links the various peoples into one is allegiance to the same sovereign. If I say that it is the monarchy which holds together the Commonwealth, I am likely to be misunderstood, for this is apt to give the impression that there is a ruling, and not merely a reigning, king. The truth is that the monarchy expresses visibly the bond of union which is in reality spiritual. Tradition, one may say again, plays a great part in human society. Other things being equal, the scion of an ancient house commands greater influence in social circles than a member of the *nouveaux riches*. Tradition often produces its effect with no consciousness on the part of the individual that it even exists. The novelist plays with this instinct when, for the entertainment of the many, he brings on his stage people of ancient lineage moving in exclusive circles, in scenes of magnificence, with old buildings, tapestries, and pictures, inherited from a glorious past. When a prince passes, our eyes turn to follow him, less because of what he is in himself than because of the long tradition which he represents. The letters "E. R." recently and the letters "G. R." now on mail carts in Canada always stir my interest. "E. R." *"Edwardus Rex."* The first of the name was *"Malleus Scotorum,"* the hammer of the Scots, who six long centuries ago broke his enemies, stood up for his kingly rights against a powerful church, and asserted for future ages in England the principle that what concerns all must be approved by all. The letters "G. R." call up a past less happy in what it did than useful as a warning; for it was a *Georgius Rex* who broke up in disaster the first British Empire. It is something to the British peoples that the symbols are preserved which link the fruits of to-day with the roots of a long ago.

The United States has nearly twice as many English-speaking people as has the whole British Empire. All these people, so far as political institutions are concerned, are in practically the same stage of political evolution. All the state legislatures have substantially the same powers and all the states share in the same manner in the federal government.   The American Commonwealth is the greatest community the world has ever seen with a uniform type of representative government over its whole vast area.   Strikingly different is the government of the British Commonwealth.   Even its sixty-five millions of peoples of European origin have an almost capricious variety of systems.   Great Britain, even half a century ago, was governed by the nobility and the upper middle class.   It was with dismay that Queen Victoria saw the late Joseph Chamberlain, a manufacturer and a supposedly extreme radical, take high office.   Soon working men, who had labored with their hands, became Cabinet ministers, and now the prime minister himself is from this social class.   The House of Commons has gained final mastery over the House of Lords, which now can delay, but cannot permanently defeat, measures not to its taste.   Democracy is in the saddle in Great Britain, but the old forms are unchanged.   There is a king; there are peers and commoners; men still pursue eagerly hereditary titles of honor; but the vitality has gone out of conservative reaction and the masses control the government. It is a far cry from the Whig Lord Palmerston of the sixties to the Lloyd George of to-day.

In other parts of the British Commonwealth the logic of environment has produced other types of constitutions. England remains immovable in that omnicompetence of Parliament which keeps all legislative power for Great Britain at Westminster. But for British states differently situated this system has proved inadequate. In 1867 Canada turned to federalism. When, more than thirty years later, in 1900, Australia, after long hesitation, adopted federalism, it was a federalism more closely akin to that of the United States than is the Canadian system. Australia took power to change its own constitution, something which, in form, Canada has not yet done. Ten years later South Africa, in a different situation, adopted for its four states a type of political union which was less a federation than a unitary state with subordinate legislatures of very limited authority. New Zealand has a single legislature; and now India, clamoring for self-government, is given a system which is half federal in that it divides authority, but in respect to the executive power is not greatly unlike that of Canada sixty years ago. The variety of systems in the British Commonwealth is accompanied by what is unknown in the United States—a variety of official languages. Federal Canada uses indifferently French or English in public affairs. South Africa uses indifferently Dutch or English.

There is no serious movement to create a federal union of all the self-governing states of the Commonwealth. The war has fostered an acute nationalism in Canada. For the moment, at least, there is no prospect of securing Canada's assent to any form of centralization which, in the slightest degree, impairs her own sovereignty. There exists, however, the machinery for consultation and cooperation. The absence of any real central authority has made the more necessary some means for discussing matters of policy which affect the British Commonwealth as a whole. In response to this need there met in 1887 the first Conference, called then the Colonial Conference, but now significantly renamed the Imperial Conference.  Since that date in every fourth year, at least, have come together representatives of all the British peoples to take counsel.  The body has no mandatory authority; it is in very truth a Conference only; but it discusses great problems and it has reached agreements and helped to mold the public opinion of all the British states.  It gives at least opportunity to the leaders to come together, and to learn to understand each other.  One can only record a melancholy regret that in 1776 no such Conference had been created.  If at that time the leaders of all the British states had been able to sit quietly round a table to discuss their differences, the story of the world might have had some happier pages.

## LECTURE VI

## THE FUTURE

In the stress of a great conflict it gives men pleasure to picture the days of peace when they may rest from their labors. It is a paradox of life that idealism flourishes most in times which are farthest from the ideal. Amid the horrors of war we picture with intense hope the joys of peace. Thus it happened that during the Great War we dreamed and hoped and, in many cases, believed in a new era which should come with victory. This idealism was sincere, and it is only a shallow view to suppose that it has failed. But now the strain of war is removed; the dirt, the brutality, the coarse obscenity are no longer in evidence; and we are not compelled in our misery to turn for comfort to the ideal. Perhaps it was thought that the new era would come more easily than could be possible. But, until hope becomes a vice and is no longer a virtue, no wise per-

son will sneer at the conviction that out of a
world struggle must come a world awaken-
ing to better ideals of well-being. The task
is difficult, and when we confront it we may
ponder the solemn words of Milton: "To
guide . . . mighty states by counsel, to conduct them from institutions of error to a
worthier discipline, to extend a provident
care to furthest shores, to watch, to foresee, to shrink from no toil, to flee all the
empty shows of opulence and power—these,
indeed, are things so arduous that, compared
with them, war is but as the play of children."

The idealism of a time of war has a cause
simple enough. Men are united in a common purpose. If in the colossal strength of
their union they can conquer the problems
of war, they feel that they can face with ease
the safer problems of peace. On these problems, however, there is not the same unity of
conviction. Society is so organized that each
class considers its safety to depend upon
alert regard for its own interests. The
wage-earner tries to get the most from the
employer, and the employer in turn fears
ruin if he yields too much to the wage-earner.

Thus the idealism of a period of war is apt to
end with the war itself, and with peace comes
a reversion to rival aims and rival interests.
It is all a part of the drama of man's life;
but because this happens the pessimist must
not imagine that he has gained an easy victory. War seems to change even the fiber of
men's minds; there is no doubt that the late
war, at least, has shattered a mass of convictions which men accepted as ultimate without reasoning on their origins. In effect,
if not in form, some political parties have
disappeared and all have been shaken. A
good many people blush to think that they
once accepted shibboleths which now they
see to have had no meaning. The pessimist
sees in this the dissolution of human society.
No doubt it is a serious thing for the con-
ventions which men have obeyed suddenly
to break down. But, if we have an ultimate
faith in man, we will believe that the break-
down means the liberation of his mind from
what was dead and oppressive, and that he
has the vitality to reorganize his effort on
better lines. Out of the *débris* of the old
system will come slowly, and no doubt with

the pain and sorrow which accompany all of man's achievement, something which to vital insight will seem to justify his sacrifices.

Unless we can face the future in this spirit there is not much in the political outlook at the present time to cheer the heart. Europe is still [April, 1920] the scene of the horrors of war, and America is not at peace with itself. On every side are unrest and suspicion. Whole peoples are suffering as they have never suffered before. Every effort of devilish ingenuity is being made to embroil the two great English-speaking nations. Perhaps humanity has learned by this time that the good triumphs only after evil has done its worst; and it may be that the very intensity of the efforts to create bitterness of feeling is proof that the dawn of a better day is near. At any rate we may regretfully admit that the task of shaping the relations of nations to make war impossible is so stern and difficult that compared with it the problems of war itself are "but as the play of children."

The two English-speaking federations in

North America became in the end partners in the Great War. There was a difference. From the first day Canada was clear in its resolve not to stand aloof, while only slowly and with reluctance did the American people see that they too must join in this struggle which had begun between nations in Europe. The difference has its roots deep in history. The American federation, as we have seen, was founded in the conviction that the republic was to give to the world a new note in political life, and that one chief condition of success would be to keep aloof from entanglement in the worn-out politics of Europe. What wonder that, when this tradition had been fixed for a century and a quarter, and when suddenly Europe burst into the flames of a mighty conflagration, there should be careful scrutiny of the issue in the United States. At the outburst of the war in 1914 I happened to be living in a watering-place where about half of the people were Americans and half of them Canadians. All felt that Germany had provoked the war and condemned her action. "You must remember, however, that this is a European war, and that we are not in it," said a young American scholar to me. The attitude of the young Canadian was in sharp contrast. He had never been taught any tradition of holding aloof from entanglements in Europe. His fear during the tremulous days just before the 4th of August, 1914, was that Britain might hold aloof. If she did, he even thought that Canada ought to declare war against Germany on her own account and do her part, whether England did or did not share in the effort to save liberty in the world.

It may be that in this contrasted attitude of mind we find one of the chief differences in the spirit of the two federations. Of all Europe, not excluding France, her own ally in the Revolution, the United States is suspicious. She has made her territory the refuge of the oppressed, and the multitudes who have flocked to her shores from Europe to find liberty have strengthened rather than weakened her conception of the dangers from European intrigues. Canada, on the other hand, has preserved a close tie with a European state, and has had a child-like belief

in this state as playing a magnanimous role
in world politics.  If, in wide circles in the
United States, everything which England
proposes or does is to be scanned with a
suspicious eye, in Canada the presumption
is that the politics of Britain are the purest,
her system the most wisely democratic, and
her statesmen the best trained and the most
high-minded of any in the world.  When the
Canadian constitution was framed, all parties were unanimous in trusting the tribunal
known as the Privy Council, which sits in
London, to say the final word when any disputes should arise as to the interpretation
of the constitution.  To this day Canadian
lawyers cling to the right of ultimate appeal
to this tribunal as a guarantee that the best
judgments will be given which human wisdom can achieve.  Thus it happened that
when Britain was involved in the war there
was not a moment's hesitation in Canada.
For what was at stake she was ready to
pledge her all, and did in the end pledge it.
In this she was not unique.  Australia and
New Zealand made sacrifices as great and
the whole British Commonwealth was united

in measure not thought, even by astute statesmen, to be possible.

Paradox lingers on the path of all our efforts, and it is certainly true that out of this unity has come a new emphasis upon the right, and, indeed, the need, of each of the nations in the Commonwealth to live its own distinct national life. The paradox is less striking than it seems. No compulsion could have produced the unity. It was rather the expression of free individuality, a consensus based upon both natural instinct and political reflection. The strain of the great effort brought to each unit a vital self-consciousness. Each was free to do what it chose; each felt that the race for victory could be won only by the trained use of every muscle; each felt that it was in honorable competition with the others. It was with a thrill of pride that Australia and Canada found that their sons ranked with the best in the intricate achievements of war. This experience quickened the growth of nationalism, and it took unexpected forms. At an earlier time the Canadian Pacific Railway, conceived and carried through by men whose fortunes and interests centered in Canada, had been an achievement which demanded recognition and the recognition which seemed most appropriate was to make three of its leading architects members of the British House of Lords. In the early stages of the war this recognition of Canada's effort by British titles of honor was accepted. Then there came a sudden outburst against it. People began to say that titles of honor, and especially hereditary titles of honor, which might be in place in an old civilization, were out of place in Canada, and the Canadian Parliament put an end to the practice.

It has not been easy for other nations to follow this growth of national life within the British Commonwealth. The United States had long since recognized the principle that the British Empire was in a fiscal sense a single state which might give what trade preferences it liked among its own members without raising any question of the rights of other countries to the treatment of the most favored nation. In this sense there was to the United States but one British nation.

In the law of belligerency there was also one. When Great Britain was at war, Canada too was at war. It was therefore puzzling to find Canada claiming definite national status and the right to speak for herself at foreign capitals, and the puzzle was increased as soon as the problems of the proposed League of Nations came under close scrutiny. When the Treaty of Peace was signed at Versailles, in 1919, the representatives of Canada, Australia, and other Dominions signed it, and in doing so became in their own right members of the League of Nations. Thus, as parties to the peace, the British Commonwealth became not one but six nations. Yet, as we have seen, in the view of the United States, and for the advantage not of the United States but of the British Commonwealth, it was regarded fiscally as a single state. It was one, too, when a question of war arose. Now, in the League of Nations it became six. On the surface political paradox could no further go.

The League of Nations has become a vexing problem in politics, and this is not the place to take sides on a great issue. If one may summarize what the League aims at, it may be covered under four chief points:

1. Publicity of treaties between states, so as to end secret obligations which may become a menace to the security of other states.

2. The creation of an international court to give judgment in cases of disputes between nations, and thus prevent recourse to war.

3. Provision for the reduction of armaments by consent of the nation or nations concerned, and guarantees for the permanence of the scale of armaments agreed upon.

4. The ending of the system of exploiting weak states by strong ones, and the putting of weak states under the ultimate guardianship of the League of Nations, with authority to give mandates to nations selected for the purpose to act as guardians of the weaker states, and under obligation to give account to the League of Nations for the discharge of the responsibility assumed.

When the opportunity to join the League of Nations came, Canada entered the League gladly and proudly. The United States, however, speaking through the Senate, held back. Once more was there in evidence the contrast in tradition of the two federations, the United States dreading entanglements in Europe, Canada feeling herself as much a European as an American state, and ready to follow where Britain led. A nation which feels that it has made a special place for itself in the world and has based its institutions on a new application of political theory naturally looks with a critical eye on proposals for adopting a common policy with other states. The outside world wondered that during the war the United States never spoke of "allies," but always of "associated powers," for the good reason that she made no treaty of alliance with the other belligerents like that between France and Britain. There was working the thought that complete identity of aim was not possible between an idealist republic and the war-worn states of Europe. Objection to joining the League of Nations thus fitted in with a vivid tradition. The United States must do nothing to guarantee political frontiers in Europe and thus embroil itself there; it must maintain its authority in respect to America, and not permit non-American nations to take part in directing policy which might conflict with the principles of the Monroe Doctrine; it must maintain the right to use its own judgment as to withdrawal from any League; above all, it must not put itself in a position of relative inferiority to any other great power.  Six votes for the British Empire with only one for the United States seemed to indicate inferior status.  So reasoned American idealism, and for the moment the United States remained out of the League.

The Canadian federation had its own idealism working to an opposite conclusion. The political movement, which we know as the American Revolution, was at first only a domestic protest in a matter of constitutional right.  When, however, the issue was once confronted, American thought took a wider range and confronted an ultimate problem of human liberty.  A year of struggle convinced Washington and his comrades in arms that they must break with a treasured past, and declare for British citizens in America complete independence of the motherland. The reluctance with which the step was taken is very marked—as marked as that with which the Pilgrim Fathers turned from their dear England to make new homes in a rough and unknown continent. The tragedy of the American Revolutionary War demonstrated the truth that it is a violation of a law of nature for a people to try to hold in a position of subordination communities of similar origin but of more recent foundation. The old have always thought that they could speak words of guiding wisdom to the young, but the young have sooner or later retorted that their manhood required them to think for themselves. The problem which Canada, the second in importance of the English-speaking states overseas, has had to solve has been not less vital than that of the American Revolution. Could Canada remain a state of the British Commonwealth and yet attain national manhood on the basis of complete political equality with Great Britain?

When the time came for making peace, Canada demanded recognition as a distinct nation, but a nation within the complex British Commonwealth. The demand was acceded to at Versailles. Possibly when M. Clémenceau so readily accepted it he had in his mind the thought that it really did not matter, since in ultimate constitutional fact the British Commonwealth was one in respect to the issues of war and peace, and separate signature of the Treaty by Canada would serve only to reenforce an obligation which the single signature by Great Britain already created. But Canada valued the point. It involved the recognition by the whole world of a political principle which the leaders of the American Revolution had believed incredible, that within a single state under a single sovereign there could be distinct nations, no one of them subordinate to any of the others, and yet linked together by ties firm enough to be strengthened, and not weakened, during the hard testing and sacrifices of war. The observer might well smile when he saw the United States so cautious and reserved in regard to assuming the obligations of the League of Nations and Canada so eager to accept them. But there was a reason. The United States, as a result of a revolution, had an assured status before the world. Canada, long regarded as a colony of Great Britain, had no such status as a nation. For this status she was willing to pay the price by assuming responsibilities as a member of the League of Nations.

Now, with the war over, the English-speaking peoples must face the whole question of world-order. The war was a war of principles. It is not manly to hurl reproaches at a defeated opponent, and this is not the time to pile up an indictment of Germany. History has given and will maintain its stern verdict. During many years Germany steadily refused to join in the movement to lessen by arbitration treaties the danger of war. The nations of the world required, she believed, leadership and, if need be, control from the strong and efficient. This she thought herself to be in a sense true of no other nation. Germany alone, as Fichte said early in the nineteenth century, had been intrusted with "the seeds of human perfection," and if Germany should fail, humanity would succumb. Thus not brotherhood, but mastery, was Germany's duty, and every step needed to secure mastery was justified. "Our troops must achieve victory. What else matters?" said a certain General von Disfürth, and he added that Germany owed explanations to no one for Louvain and Reims: "There is nothing for us to justify and nothing for us to explain away." Germany was to rule the world for the world's good, and, since the end was noble, all means to secure the end were permissible. Even the German sword had its hymn: "Day after day I ride aloft on the shadowy horse in the valley of cypresses, and as I ride I draw forth the life-blood from every enemy's son that dares to dispute my path. . . . Am I not the flaming messenger of the Almighty?"

The alternative to the German conception is to consider mankind a brotherhood, a family of potential equals, in which the strong will help and encourage the weak and try to raise them to the level of the highest. It is no doubt true that the greater part of man's record tells a story far other than this—a story of the robbery, the enforced servitude of the weak by the strong.

Only a bold nation could plead "not guilty" to the charge of having played some part in this melancholy aspect of the human drama, and the culmination was a world war in which perished something like ten million human beings. During the agony of this struggle men asked themselves whether this must always be so, and the heart of mankind said "No!" White men and brown men and yellow men and black men all gave the same aspiring answer. No one of them was willing to be under the heel of the other; all, as the world unrest of to-day shows, had aspirations to be free and independent. There could be no one great and strong state dominating all the others for their good. Different types of men must evolve differing types of state. They would have misunderstandings and rivalries. Always would there be the danger of armed strife, and to prevent a renewed and even greater catastrophe some means must be devised of making not Force but Justice respected and obeyed. And this was the call for a League of Nations.

The subject lends itself, without doubt,

to the platitudes and perorations of easy-going optimism. In eras of upheaval men have loved to dwell upon vague theories of abstract right, and the exhortation of Mirabeau has always some pertinence, that if heed is given to Duties, Rights will take care of themselves. In all idealism there is the perennial danger of mere pedantry. Some who talk of the rights of a people to self-determination seem to imply that every people has the capacity to devise and conduct a government, which is not true. Perhaps Mirabeau was right when he told the French National Assembly to think only of duties. Rights are privileges. Duties relate to responsibility. More and more does the modern state within its own border organize effort to protect the helpless and restrain the strong who seek to do evil. In a civilized society no one is allowed to take the law into his own hands, and the decent people unite to support the forces of order. Churches and individuals make great sacrifices in order to uplift remote peoples by missionary effort. It is not too much to hope that such labor can be carried beyond private effort, and that nations will unite in sacrifices to make the world a decent place in which to live.

Careless optimism has proved baneful in the past and may easily do so again. A great empire has been laid in the dust, and yet its sixty million people are not wholly crushed. From it have been taken not merely Alsace-Lorraine in the West, now protected by the powerful arm of France, but Polish provinces in the east, with no protector but the newly organized republic of Poland, which has hardly yet escaped from the disorder and incompetence due to a tragic past. Germany looks upon these Slav peoples as "a malleable medley of incompetents," and feels in regard to her lost Polish provinces what the United States would feel if by some stroke of ill-fortune Mexico should recover control of Texas. That Germany accepts her loss as final is hardly conceivable. She has a vast population which, however disunited in respect to forms of government, is united in feeling contempt for the Pole, and in a resolve to leave no German population under his domination. In seeing that this is true we need not read into the German mind any sinister desire to revive the old dream of world-power. That ambition is gone, probably forever. But there remains, even if we look no farther than the borders of the old Germany, enough of bitter race hatreds and rivalries to make armed strife at any time possible, and such a fire is likely to spread. What is the use of trying to reconstruct a shattered civilization if it is only again to be menaced steadily by the same old destructive forces, unchecked and unrestrained? The task would be too disheartening. Hope and courage need some new note to cheer them on. And the note that has in it vital promise is found in the unity of aim and in the cooperation of the two English-speaking peoples.

At this moment these two peoples are the strongest force ever known in human history. In natural resources they surpass any measure which can have been imagined in earlier ages. They have coal and iron, gold and silver, timber and rich agricultural lands, and climatic conditions the most suitable for human effort. They have the power to say of evil forces working in international affairs that they shall not prevail, power to hold malignancy in check, power to restrain ignoble greed among the nations for territory and plunder. It is true of each of the two great English-speaking states that they have no unachieved ambitions to make them discontented and restless in respect to things as they now stand in the world. Germany was conscious of power within herself; she felt that the acknowledged scene of her dominance was not adequate to her capacity; and she waged war in order to enlarge her borders. There is no temptation for the English-speaking peoples to attempt anything of the kind. They will not give up what the fortune of history has brought to them; but they desire nothing that anyone else holds. Neither of them has any ambitions which menace the other. They speak the same language and can understand each other's thoughts. They are both great trading and industrial nations. Both know perfectly well that peace is their highest interest. If they stand together for human well-being, they can at least make the world safe from the menace of great wars.

The world has had many experiences of plans to avert war, and we shall not be wise to think that after so many failures a final remedy is to be found. In the Middle Ages the Pope, the universal spiritual father, was to be the tribunal to which his believing children were to bring disputes for settlement, without wars. Yet war continued to flourish. It flourished with even deadlier pertinacity when some nations broke away from the papacy and the terrible wars of religion followed. Dynastic wars came in the wake of religious wars. Then in a revolutionary age old dynasties broke down, and a Napoleon offered peace to the world on the basis of his own power as a soldier to hold all others in check. Napoleon fell, and a holy alliance of European rulers, who should act toward each other as Christian brothers, seemed to furnish the best promise of enduring peace. And a hundred years after the creation of this cure for the ills of nations came a World War, with destruction and horror on a scale surpassing anything in the previous history of mankind. It is not an inspiring record, but it has its conspicuous moral—that no tribunal, no mechanism of procedure, will save the world from war. Only the friendly spirit, the belief of whole peoples in each other's integrity, will create the conditions which will insure peace.

If the English-speaking peoples cannot learn this mutual confidence, we may indeed sorrow for the future of mankind. The outlook of a people is molded to an extent great, but not capable of analysis, by its traditional modes of thought, by the attitude toward life of its classic writers, by clearly defined and explicit standards handed on from one generation to another. The Puritanism of England of the age of Cromwell passed into the fiber of the New England which sprang from it, and to this day it shapes the moral standards of millions of Americans who know not from what source has come the fashioning of their beliefs. The devout Catholic acquires from the long past of a Rome of which he may know nothing the traditional beliefs and motives which touch his dearest hopes and affections. Thus is it that tradition makes the present the child of the past. Peoples with differing traditions find it hard to understand one another. The body of French tradition is different from that of Germany. The classic leaders and thinkers of one country are not those of the other, and it is not easy for a Frenchman and a German to attain unity of outlook. Montaigne may have molded the thought of one, Luther that of the other. There is above all the barrier of language. If all Germany spoke French or all France spoke German, we should probably find strange and unexpected results in the attitude of the two peoples toward each other. Friendliness might not at first increase, for members of the same family often quarrel because they understand each other so completely, but each country would know the thoughts of the other. The recent war taught the world that the German language concealed from understanding by other nations a mentality well-nigh impervious to influences from without.

In the light of such facts one may be pardoned for asking again what hope there is for agreement among other nations, if the two English-speaking nations cannot learn to understand each other. From the same source came their most precious traditions, their language, their literature, their attitude toward life. They are creative peoples. Wherever they go they bring curiosity and energy to bear on what nature offers to man's effort; and industry and commerce spring up from this turning of nature's resources to the service of man. Both are self-reliant and masterful, but the masterfulness does not take the form of a desire to enslave others. It is the masterfulness of equals in free competition. Both have made great sacrifices to abolish the institution of slavery, with man owning man as property. Freedom of speech, diversity of religious beliefs, but complete tolerance for all, a political system based on appeals to the judgment of the many—these are common to both peoples. Both have profoundly influenced the political life of the modern world. England has played in history the role of creating and handing on to others representative institutions now accepted in every continent;

the United States has led in giving votes to the many and in forwarding that democracy, so potent for good if wise in spirit, so malignant in its working if the spirit is evil.

We are tempted not less in domestic than in international affairs to satisfy ourselves with creating machinery, without taking the needed care to furnish the power which will make the machinery perform its proper tasks. In politics the vital thing is not the form but the spirit. A despotism, indefensible in the principles which it embodies, may yet, if inspired by sanity and wisdom, effect beneficent ends, while, on the other hand, a holy alliance, become the tool of designing selfishness, may lure nations on to irretrievable disaster. There is no magic which will make a League of Nations or a democracy bring about good rather than evil, other than the magic of intelligent and high resolve expressed in energetic action. The noblest ideals may be perverted to base ends. The militarist ambitions of the soldier caste in Germany were concealed behind some of the best aspirations of a political society. The Germany which Bismarck created had

universal suffrage, so that every man seemed
assured of political rights; it had a costly
and efficient system of state education, so
that no one need be illiterate; it had pen-
sions for old age; it cared for the indigent,
and boasted that in its crowded centers
there were decency and comfort unknown
in the slums of London or New York. Yet
behind these good things lurked the spirit
which made force its god and despotic power
its end, and a world disaster followed. The
German who read deeply enough to see
what all this really meant was yet impotent
to check it, for he was confronted by a powerful and ruthless hierarchy which brooked
no interference with its aims.

In moments of gloom we are tempted to
think that the forces of evil are more readily
organized than those of good; but it is not
really so. Since evil is selfish it carries with
it the seeds of disintegration. Any system
based upon the denial of fundamental human right is weak. Democracy with all its
faults is stronger than despotism. Despotism means the power of one over the many
and cannot be based on any human right,

while democracy asserts the right on the part of the many to think and act for themselves. A democratic society, however drab and commonplace it may seem, rests nevertheless on a sound basis. What it needs is leadership which it can trust, leadership which will appeal to the fine things lurking in man's nature and not to the evil things also lurking there; it needs direction by the best, and not by the worst, elements in our society. Some who think themselves initiated and in touch with reality will shrug their shoulders and say that the thing is impossible, that there is no room in politics as now organized for the refined and the educated. It is an age-old cynicism. Su T'ang Pu, an ancient Chinese poet, expressed it in his bitter reflection on the birth of a son: "Families when a child is born want it to be intelligent; I, through intelligence, having wrecked my whole life, only hope the boy may prove ignorant and stupid; then he will crown a tranquil life by becoming a Cabinet minister." But the cynicism does not express truth. The man who made the greatest personal impress on his generation,

Theodore Roosevelt, came out of the circle which thought it degrading for a gentleman to face the rough-and-tumble of politics. I say nothing of his policies, which may have been right or mistaken, but he made himself felt beyond what was possible to a man of coarser type. Education, intelligence, and refinement, if linked with simplicity of character, are assets, and not handicaps, in the leadership of the masses. England has one lesson to teach which other democratic societies have not yet learned—that the best and ablest in a nation's life can find in its politics the widest sphere for their ambitions.

John Stuart Mill described democracy as "collective mediocrity." We might say the same of an army; indeed, of mankind as a whole. But this collective mediocrity followed an inspired Lincoln in civil affairs; and the masses in France followed and believed in the greatest military genius whom the world has ever known. The multitude has the capacity to recognize a man when it sees him. A distracted world is clamoring for leaders who can say the word of wisdom because they have intelligence trained for their tasks. We confront far-reaching problems of capital and labor. Who but an educated man can understand them? Cobbett defined capital as "money taken from the laboring classes, which, being given to army tailors and such like, enables them to keep fox hounds and trace their descent from the Normans." There is cynical cleverness in the definition, but it does not go far to explain one of the most intricate problems of our present society. One condition of a real belief in liberty is a prior belief in man, in his capacity and willingness to see and follow the good, else would liberty be only the license to the brute to gratify his own appetites. When we claim the right for the individual to judge for himself we imply the confidence that in the long run he will judge wisely and who can help him to do so if it is not the trained and the educated?

There is ground for a chastened optimism when we look out on the world. The free English-speaking peoples have power. Let that be written in the forefront of our hopes. For more than a hundred years there has been no bloody strife between the two divi-

sions. The long record of peace among some
of the great nations takes a very wide sweep
which seems to indicate the working of
forces hidden to our consciousness. In the
hands of five nations is to-day the destiny
of the world. The nations are the United
States, Britain, France, Italy, and Japan;
and it is noteworthy that no one of them
has for more than a century drawn the sword
against any of the others. They represent
the dominant power in all the continents.
Hardly a dog dare bark should they say the
word of prohibition—and among themselves
they have loved and long preserved peace.
This is a story full of promise. Of promise, too, though often not so regarded, is a
part of the record of the nations which have
been at war. We look upon the settlements
made at Vienna in 1815 as having contained
the seed of future strife. Yet they so endured that for forty years there was no serious war in Europe. Nothing is clearer in
the history of Europe during the last hundred years than that the hand of justice is
strong to remove the causes of war. During that period the Turk has been at the

root of half the wars of Europe. His is a terrible record. His brutal tyranny mangled the very souls of the peoples of southeastern Europe, and recovery from their degradation will take centuries. The Turk caused the Crimean war. He has been the source of most of the trouble in the Balkans. He brought Russia and Great Britain face to face with war in 1878. More than once did his presence in Europe bring Russia and Austria to the verge of war. In his fatuous folly, after Italy and the Balkan states had nearly destroyed him, he plunged into the last great war. He has long been the key to European unrest. He ruled without justice. Now, with his malevolent power gone, the ferment of Europe will tend to disappear. Other modern wars have been due to a type of injustice which broad statesmanship could correct. It was injustice in Italy that brought Austria and France to war in 1859. It was slavery that brought civil war in the United States. It was the denial of nationalism, in itself a sound principle of political life, which brought the era of war in central Europe between 1864 and 1871.

With the alien oppressor removed and the rights of nationality now recognized, most of the causes of recent wars disappear. It will take time for peoples suddenly freed to find their natural equilibrium, but war will tend steadily to decrease if nations will recognize decent standards of justice, and the free nations must assert these standards.

It is a sound maxim of individual conduct to keep friendships in repair, and the maxim is sound, too, for nations. There is no ground for suspicion and antagonism between the English-speaking peoples. They are rivals in trade, but so also are persons who share a common citizenship and patriotism. If they will cultivate friendship and rebuke the breeders of strife, they can lead the world with power irresistible. To be champions of justice in the world, they must correct the injustices within their own borders. Every nation has some great vexing problem to test the vitality of its spirit of justice. Great Britain has the problem of Ireland, the United States that of the negro. Both are profoundly difficult and neither is capable of any ready-made or mechanical solution.

The thing to make sure of is that remedial processes are working vigorously. There is no harm in one nation criticizing another and pointing out defects. What does harm is malignancy, the devilish desire to create discord. School-books foster it when they instill into the minds of the children of to-day the worn-out passions of conflicts long since ended. The press fosters it when it places undue emphasis upon differences and forgets deeper causes for agreement. Individuals foster it when they permit themselves to speak of other nations in terms of reproach and contempt. To keep friendships in repair we must nourish the methods of friendship.

We stand to-day at the beginning of a new era for mankind. As never before in human history are minds unsettled and old methods of action and persuasion abandoned. We confront in millions suspicion and discontent, so strident that timid souls think all is lost and abandon hope for human society. But, unless we give up belief in mankind, this is not the note of true manhood. Rather is the call of to-day to new

faith and, on the basis of faith, hope. The
law of sacrifice is the law of human progress.
There is a sacrifice or, rather, a retribution,
which is the Nemesis of national misconduct,
and Nemesis has now demanded her full por-
tion. The nations were selfish and greedy;
the rich were arrogant and the poor were
oppressed; there were dreadful sores in the
body politic; and the screaming horror of
war was, in part at least, nature's healing.
But there were other sacrifices than those
which purifying justice demanded. Millions of brave men, the pride of the nations
from which they sprang, confronted death
with firm and sad constancy, not because they
believed that they must die to expiate their
country's sin, but because they were willing
to die as Christ died, to save mankind by a
glorious obedience to the highest call of manhood. The world stands in the light of that
stupendous sacrifice, and faith in what is involved in manhood makes us believe that the
sacrifices cannot have been in vain.

Here on the American continent two
English-speaking federations, heirs to the
liberty of all the ages, are living side by side

in the vast expanse of their territories, and are called to take their share of responsibility for human well-being. The older federation has no antagonism to the younger. The younger has copied the older in much that it has done. The older, a new type of political society in a new sphere, with its own tests and standards, shows a proud independence of what the rest of the world may think. The younger is a member of a world-wide union; it is tied by convictions and sympathy to an ancient state; and it is following the traditions of that state. It would be the pride of Canada to play some worthy part in bringing closer together this ancient state and the newer society in America. She owes much to both; in a deep sense she is a pupil of both; she has shared the burdens of both in the hard field of war; and she is linked to both by fresh memories of its stern cost.

Thus my last word, a Briton, a Canadian, an alien speaking in the United States, is this, that there is something noble to be done to save the world, that our two peoples represent dominant power in the world, and that they can, if they will, achieve a mighty thing for mankind. The sick world needs the support of the strongest arms. Much ought to be done, and what ought to be done can be done. "What desertion is for the soldier, pessimism is for the civilian," said a French writer during the war. The war is over, and the problems of peace are before us. During war faith made us spurn any thought that we could be beaten. It is treason to mankind to give up hope that similar endurance and courage can solve our problems of peace.

17 MY